Southern DESSERTS

Southern DESSERTS

Classic Recipes *for* Every Occasion

hm | books

 hm|books

EXECUTIVE VICE PRESIDENT/CCO Brian Hart Hoffman
VICE PRESIDENT/EDITORIAL Cindy Smith Cooper
ART DIRECTOR Cailyn Haynes

TASTE OF THE SOUTH EDITORIAL
EDITOR Brooke Michael Bell
CREATIVE DIRECTOR/PHOTOGRAPHY Mac Jamieson
ASSOCIATE EDITOR Josh Miller
EDITORIAL ASSISTANT Alexa Bode
COPY EDITORS Maria Parker Hopkins, Whitney Law
CONTRIBUTING COPY EDITOR Donna Baldone
STYLISTS Amy Hannum, Mary Beth Stillwell
CONTRIBUTING STYLISTS Malinda Kay Nichols,
Anna Pollock Rayner, Katherine Tucker
SENIOR PHOTOGRAPHERS John O'Hagan, Marcy Black Simpson
PHOTOGRAPHERS Sarah Arrington, William Dickey,
Stephanie Welbourne, Kamin Williams
CONTRIBUTING PHOTOGRAPHER Kimberly Finkel Davis
TEST KITCHEN DIRECTOR Janice Ritter
EXECUTIVE CHEF Rebecca Treadwell
TEST KITCHEN PROFESSIONALS Allene Arnold, Melissa L. Brinley,
Kathleen Kanen, Janet Lambert, Aimee Bishop Lindsey,
Anna Theoktisto, Loren Wood
CONTRIBUTING TEST KITCHEN PROFESSIONALS Rachael Daylong,
Jane Drennen, Virginia Hornbuckle, Chantel Lambeth
TEST KITCHEN ASSISTANT Anita Simpson Spain
SENIOR DIGITAL IMAGING SPECIALIST Delisa McDaniel
DIGITAL IMAGING SPECIALIST Clark Densmore
MULTIMEDIA DIRECTOR Bart Clayton
ONLINE MARKETING MANAGER Eric Bush
ONLINE EDITOR Victoria Phillips

hm
hoffmanmedia

PRESIDENT Phyllis Hoffman DePiano
EXECUTIVE VICE PRESIDENT/COO Eric W. Hoffman
EXECUTIVE VICE PRESIDENT/CCO Brian Hart Hoffman
EXECUTIVE VICE PRESIDENT/CFO G. Marc Neas
VICE PRESIDENT/FINANCE Michael Adams
VICE PRESIDENT/DIGITAL MEDIA Jon Adamson
VICE PRESIDENT/MANUFACTURING Greg Baugh
VICE PRESIDENT/EDITORIAL Cindy Smith Cooper
VICE PRESIDENT/CONSUMER MARKETING Silvia Rider
VICE PRESIDENT/ADMINISTRATION Lynn Lee Terry

Hoffman Media
1900 International Park Drive, Suite 50
Birmingham, Alabama 35243
hoffmanmedia.com

ISBN # 978-1-940772-09-7

Printed in Mexico

Cover recipe on page 31
Photography by Kamin Williams/Photo Styling by Anna Pollock Rayner

CONTENTS

INTRODUCTION

The gentle whir of the mixer; the warmth of a cake pan through an oven mitt; the aroma of vanilla, butter, and sugar heavy in the air—these simple pleasures foretell the promise of sweet rewards from the kitchen.

IN THE SOUTH, dessert is the highlight of every occasion. From birthdays and weddings to holidays and weeknight suppers, no gathering is complete without a sweet ending. We're known for our showstoppers like meringue-topped pies and magnificently frosted layer cakes as well as our humble fruit-filled cobblers and luscious puddings.

The best part of dessert is sharing a bite with family and friends. Dessert is—as it should be— always at the center of any Southern celebration.

Let this delicious collection of heirloom recipes and modern takes on classics be your guide to making sweet memories throughout the year.

CAKES
and
CUPCAKES

MAPLE-FROSTED CUPCAKES

YIELD: 1½ DOZEN CUPCAKES

CUPCAKES

2 cups cake flour
1 cup sugar
1 teaspoon baking powder
½ teaspoon salt
½ teaspoon baking soda
2 large eggs, lightly beaten
1 cup whole buttermilk
½ cup canola oil
2 teaspoons vanilla extract

FROSTING

½ cup unsalted butter
½ cup firmly packed light brown
  sugar
⅓ cup maple syrup
3 cups confectioners' sugar
2 tablespoons whole buttermilk
½ teaspoon vanilla extract

Garnish: chopped candied pecans

Preheat oven to 350°. Line 18 muffin cups with paper liners. Lightly spray liners with nonstick cooking spray. Set aside.

FOR CUPCAKES: In a large bowl, whisk together flour, sugar, baking powder, salt, and baking soda. Make a well in center of dry ingredients. Add eggs, whisking to combine. Gradually add buttermilk and canola oil, whisking until combined. Stir in vanilla. Beat at medium speed with an electric mixer until smooth, approximately 2 minutes. Divide batter evenly among prepared muffin cups, filling each three-fourths full.

Bake until a wooden pick inserted in center comes out clean, approximately 20 minutes. Let cool in pans 10 minutes. Remove from pans, and let cool completely on wire racks.

FOR FROSTING: In a small saucepan, bring butter, brown sugar, and syrup to a boil over medium-high heat, stirring constantly until sugar dissolves, approximately 4 minutes. Remove from heat, and let cool.

In a large bowl, add cooled sugar mixture. Gradually add confectioners' sugar, beating at medium speed with an electric mixer until smooth. Add buttermilk and vanilla. Beat at high speed until smooth and spreadable, approximately 3 minutes. Thin with additional buttermilk, if needed. Spread frosting over cupcakes. Garnish with pecans, if desired.

VANILLA POUND CAKE

YIELD: 8 TO 10 SERVINGS

3	large eggs
¼	cup whole milk
2	teaspoons vanilla extract
1½	cups cake flour
¾	cup sugar
1	teaspoon baking powder
¼	teaspoon salt
¾	cup unsalted butter, softened
4	cups sliced fresh nectarines
1	cup fresh blackberries
1	cup fresh blueberries
¼	cup honey
2	tablespoons almond-flavored liqueur
1	teaspoon orange zest
Sweetened whipped cream	

Preheat oven to 350°. Spray a 9x5-inch loaf pan with nonstick baking spray with flour. Set aside.

In a medium bowl, whisk together eggs, milk, and vanilla. In a large bowl, stir together flour, sugar, baking powder, and salt. Add butter and half of egg mixture to flour mixture, beating at low speed with an electric mixer until combined. Increase speed to medium-high. Beat until fluffy, approximately 1 minute, stopping occasionally to scrape sides of bowl. Add remaining egg mixture, ¼ cup at a time, beating well after each addition. Spoon batter in prepared pan.

Bake until a wooden pick inserted in center comes out clean, approximately 1 hour. Let cool in pan 10 minutes. Remove from pan, and let cool completely on a wire rack. Cut into slices.

In a medium bowl, combine nectarines, blackberries, blueberries, honey, liqueur, and zest. Let stand 5 minutes. Spoon over cake; top with whipped cream.

STRAWBERRY-BUTTERMILK CUPCAKES

YIELD: 2 DOZEN CUPCAKES

CUPCAKES

½ cup unsalted butter, softened
1 cup sugar
2 large eggs
1 cup whole buttermilk
1 teaspoon vanilla extract
2 cups cake flour
1 teaspoon baking powder
1 teaspoon baking soda
¾ teaspoon salt
2 cups chopped fresh strawberries

ICING

4 ounces cream cheese, softened
¼ cup unsalted butter, softened
½ cup chopped fresh strawberries
1 teaspoon orange zest
1 teaspoon fresh orange juice
6 cups confectioners' sugar

Preheat oven to 350°. Line 24 muffin cups with paper liners. Lightly spray liners with nonstick cooking spray. Set aside.

FOR CUPCAKES: In a large bowl, beat butter and sugar at medium speed with an electric mixer until fluffy, stopping occasionally to scrape sides of bowl. Add eggs, one at a time, beating well after each addition. Reduce mixer speed to low. Add buttermilk and vanilla, beating just until combined.

In a small bowl, stir together flour, baking powder, baking soda, and salt. Gradually add flour mixture to butter mixture, beating just until combined. Fold in strawberries. Divide batter evenly among prepared muffin cups.

Bake until a wooden pick inserted in center comes out clean, approximately 20 minutes. Let cool in pans 10 minutes. Remove from pans, and let cool completely on wire racks.

FOR ICING: In the work bowl of a food processor, combine cream cheese, butter, strawberries, and orange zest and juice. Process until smooth. Transfer mixture to a large bowl.

Gradually add confectioners' sugar, beating at low speed with an electric mixer until combined. Beat at high speed until fluffy, approximately 2 minutes. Spread icing on cooled cupcakes.

PEANUT BUTTER CAKE

YIELD: 1 (9-INCH) 3-LAYER CAKE

1   cup butter, softened
2   cups sugar
3   large eggs
3   cups self-rising flour
⅛   teaspoon salt
1   cup sour cream
¼   cup whole milk
1   teaspoon vanilla extract

2   cups creamy peanut butter
¼   cup confectioners' sugar
2   cups heavy whipping cream
⅛   teaspoon salt

Garnish: roasted salted peanuts, chopped

Preheat oven to 350°. Spray 3 (9-inch) round cake pans with nonstick baking spray with flour. Line bottoms of pans with parchment paper; spray with nonstick baking spray with flour. Set aside.

FOR CAKE: In a large bowl, beat butter and sugar at medium speed with an electric mixer until fluffy, stopping occasionally to scrape sides of bowl. Add eggs, one at a time, beating well after each addition.

In a medium bowl, whisk together flour and salt. In another medium bowl, whisk together sour cream, milk, and vanilla. With mixer on low speed, add flour mixture to butter mixture in thirds, alternating with sour cream mixture, beginning and ending with flour mixture. Beat until combined. Divide batter evenly among prepared pans. Tap pans on counter twice to remove air bubbles.

Bake until a wooden pick inserted in center comes out clean, approximately 25 minutes. Let cool in pans 10 minutes. Remove from pans, and let cool completely on wire racks.

FOR FROSTING: In a large bowl, beat peanut butter and confectioners' sugar at medium speed with an electric mixer until combined. Add cream and salt, beating until mixture begins to thicken. Increase speed to high; beat until thickened. Spread frosting between layers and on top and sides of cake. Garnish with peanuts, if desired.

TEXAS SHEET CAKE

YIELD: 12 TO 14 SERVINGS

CAKE

½   **cup butter**
2   **cups sugar**
1   **cup water**
½   **cup canola oil**
½   **cup whole buttermilk**
2   **large eggs, lightly beaten**
1   **teaspoon vanilla extract**
2   **cups all-purpose flour**
⅓   **cup natural unsweetened cocoa powder**
1   **teaspoon ground cinnamon**
1   **teaspoon baking soda**
¼   **teaspoon salt**

FROSTING

½   **cup butter**
⅓   **cup whole milk**
1   **(16-ounce) package confectioners' sugar**
⅓   **cup natural unsweetened cocoa powder**
¼   **teaspoon ground cinnamon**
1   **teaspoon vanilla extract**
¼   **teaspoon salt**

1   **cup toasted pecans, chopped**

Preheat oven to 400°. Spray a 15x10-inch jelly-roll pan with nonstick baking spray with flour. Set aside.

FOR CAKE: In a large microwave-safe bowl, place butter. Microwave on high until melted, approximately 1 minute. Add sugar, 1 cup water, canola oil, buttermilk, eggs, and vanilla. Beat at medium speed with an electric mixer until combined.

In a medium bowl, sift together flour, cocoa, cinnamon, baking soda, and salt. With mixer on low speed, gradually add flour mixture to sugar mixture, stopping occasionally to scrape sides of bowl. Beat just until combined. Spread batter in prepared pan.

Bake until a wooden pick inserted in center comes out clean, approximately 20 minutes.

Let cool in pan 5 minutes.

FOR FROSTING: In a large microwave-safe bowl, combine butter and milk. Microwave on high until butter is melted, approximately 1 minute.

Sift confectioners' sugar, cocoa, and cinnamon over butter mixture. Add vanilla and salt. Beat at low speed with an electric mixer until well combined. Spread frosting over warm cake. Sprinkle with pecans. Let cool completely on a wire rack.

HONEY-ORANGE LOAF CAKES

YIELD: 4 (5X3-INCH) LOAVES

CAKE

- 1¾ cups cake flour
- 1 cup sugar
- 2 teaspoons baking powder
- ¼ teaspoon salt
- ½ cup vegetable oil
- ½ cup fresh orange juice
- 2 tablespoons honey
- 4 large egg whites
- 2 tablespoons confectioners' sugar

GLAZE

- 2 cups confectioners' sugar
- ¼ cup fresh orange juice
- 2 tablespoons honey

Preheat oven to 350°. Spray 4 (5x3-inch) loaf pans with nonstick baking spray with flour. Set aside.

FOR CAKE: In a large bowl, sift together flour, sugar, baking powder, and salt. Add oil, orange juice, and honey, whisking until smooth.

In a small bowl, using clean beaters, beat egg whites at high speed with an electric mixer until soft peaks form. Gradually add confectioners' sugar, beating until stiff peaks form. Gently fold into batter. Divide batter evenly among prepared pans.

Bake until a wooden pick inserted in center comes out clean, 20 to 25 minutes. Let cool in pans 10 minutes. Remove from pans, and let cool completely on wire racks.

FOR GLAZE: In a large bowl, whisk together confectioners' sugar, orange juice, and honey until smooth. Drizzle over cooled cakes.

PEANUT BUTTER SWIRLED BUNDT

YIELD: 8 TO 10 SERVINGS

CAKE

1	cup butter, softened
1½	cups sugar
3	large eggs
2	cups self-rising flour
¼	teaspoon salt
¾	cup whole milk
1	teaspoon vanilla extract
¼	cup natural unsweetened cocoa powder
½	cup creamy peanut butter

PEANUT BUTTER GLAZE

1	cup confectioners' sugar, sifted
¼	cup creamy peanut butter
2	tablespoons whole milk
1	tablespoon dark corn syrup

CHOCOLATE GLAZE

1	cup confectioners' sugar, sifted
1	tablespoon natural unsweetened cocoa powder
5	teaspoons whole milk, divided
2	teaspoons dark corn syrup

Preheat oven to 350°. Spray a 10- to 15-cup Bundt pan with nonstick baking spray with flour. Set aside.

FOR CAKE: In a large bowl, beat butter and sugar at medium speed with an electric mixer until fluffy, stopping occasionally to scrape sides of bowl. Add eggs, one at a time, beating well after each addition. In a medium bowl, whisk together flour and salt. With mixer on low speed, add flour mixture to butter mixture in thirds, alternating with milk, beginning and ending with flour mixture. Add vanilla, beating to combine.

In a medium bowl, place cocoa. Spoon half of batter over cocoa, whisking slowly until combined. Add peanut butter to remaining batter in large bowl; beat at low speed with an electric mixer until combined. Drop heaping tablespoons of batter into prepared pan, alternating between peanut butter and chocolate mixtures. Using a knife, pull blade back and forth through batter to swirl. Tap pan on counter twice to remove air bubbles.

Bake until a wooden pick inserted near center comes out clean, approximately 40 minutes. Let cool in pan 15 minutes. Invert onto a wire rack, and let cool completely. Place cake on a serving plate.

FOR PEANUT BUTTER GLAZE: In a medium bowl, whisk together confectioners' sugar, peanut butter, milk, and corn syrup until smooth. Spoon glaze into a small resealable plastic bag. (Do not seal bag.) Snip a small hole in one corner of bag. Drizzle over cake.

FOR CHOCOLATE GLAZE: In a medium bowl, whisk together confectioners' sugar, cocoa, 3 teaspoons milk, and corn syrup until smooth, adding remaining milk, 1 teaspoon at a time, if needed. Spoon glaze into a small resealable plastic bag. (Do not seal bag.) Snip a small hole in one corner of bag. Drizzle over cake. Let stand until glazes are set, approximately 20 minutes.

LORD BALTIMORE CAKE

YIELD: 1 (8-INCH) 3-LAYER CAKE

CAKE

- 3   cups all-purpose flour
- 1½   cups sugar
- 1   tablespoon baking powder
- ½   teaspoon salt
- ¾   cup butter, cut into pieces and softened
- 1½   cups whole milk
- 6   large egg yolks
- 1   teaspoon vanilla extract

FROSTING

- 1   cup plus 3 tablespoons sugar, divided
- ⅓   cup water
- 1   tablespoon light corn syrup
- ⅛   teaspoon salt
- 4   large egg whites
- ¼   teaspoon cream of tartar
- 1   teaspoon vanilla extract

FILLING

- 1   cup finely chopped pecans
- 1   tablespoon butter
- ¼   teaspoon salt
- 2   cups frosting, divided
- 1   cup sweetened flaked coconut, divided
- 6   tablespoons cherry preserves, divided

Preheat oven to 350°. Spray 3 (8-inch) round cake pans with nonstick baking spray with flour. Set aside.

FOR CAKE: In a large bowl, combine flour, sugar, baking powder, and salt. Add butter and milk; beat at low speed with an electric mixer until combined. Increase speed to high, and beat 2 minutes, stopping occasionally to scrape sides of bowl. Reduce speed to medium. Add egg yolks, one at a time, beating well after each addition. Stir in vanilla. Divide batter evenly among prepared pans.

Bake until a wooden pick inserted in center comes out clean, approximately 25 minutes. Let cool in pans 10 minutes. Remove from pans, and let cool completely on wire racks.

FOR FROSTING: In a small heavy saucepan, combine 1 cup sugar, ⅓ cup water, corn syrup, and salt; swirl saucepan to moisten sugar. Bring to a boil over medium-high heat, stirring just until sugar dissolves. Cook, without stirring, until a candy thermometer reads 238°, approximately 5 minutes. Remove from heat. Meanwhile, in the bowl of a stand mixer using the whisk attachment, beat egg whites and cream of tartar at high speed until foamy. Gradually add remaining 3 tablespoons sugar, beating just until soft peaks form. With mixer on medium speed, slowly pour hot sugar syrup into egg whites. Increase speed to high; beat just until stiff peaks form. Beat in vanilla.

FOR FILLING: On a small rimmed baking sheet, combine pecans, butter, and salt. Bake at 350°, stirring occasionally, until pecans are toasted, approximately 6 minutes. Let cool completely.

On a cake plate, place one cake layer; spread top with 1 cup frosting. Sprinkle with ½ cup pecans and ½ cup coconut. Drop half of preserves by teaspoonfuls over coconut. Repeat with another cake layer, 1 cup frosting, and remaining pecans, coconut, and preserves. Top with remaining cake layer. Spread remaining frosting over top and sides of cake. Let stand at least 30 minutes before serving.

TRES LECHES CAKE

YIELD: 10 TO 12 SERVINGS

1   cup butter, softened
2   cups sugar
4   large eggs
1   teaspoon vanilla extract
3   cups all-purpose flour
1   teaspoon baking powder
½   teaspoon baking soda
¼   teaspoon salt
1½ cups whole buttermilk
3   cups heavy whipping cream,
    divided
1   (14-ounce) can sweetened
    condensed milk
1   (5-ounce) can evaporated milk
½   cup confectioners' sugar

Garnish: fresh raspberries, fresh mint

Preheat oven to 350°. Spray a 13x9-inch baking pan with nonstick baking spray with flour. Set aside.

In a large bowl, beat butter and sugar at medium speed with an electric mixer until fluffy, stopping occasionally to scrape sides of bowl. Add eggs, one at a time, beating well after each addition. Beat in vanilla.

In a medium bowl, stir together flour, baking powder, baking soda, and salt. With mixer on low speed, add flour mixture to butter mixture in thirds, alternating with buttermilk, beginning and ending with flour mixture. Beat until well combined. Spread batter evenly in prepared pan.

Bake until a wooden pick inserted in center comes out clean, 30 to 35 minutes. Loosely cover with aluminum foil during last 10 minutes to prevent excess browning, if necessary.

In a medium bowl, whisk together 1 cup cream, condensed milk, and evaporated milk. Using a wooden skewer or wooden pick, poke holes in warm cake. Slowly pour cream mixture over cake. Let cool completely in pan. Refrigerate until ready to serve.

In a medium bowl, beat remaining 2 cups cream at medium-high speed with an electric mixer until soft peaks form. Add confectioners' sugar, beating until stiff peaks form. Spread whipped cream on top of cake. Garnish with raspberries and mint, if desired.

CARROT CAKE WITH GINGER-CREAM CHEESE ICING

YIELD: 1 (9-INCH) 3-LAYER CAKE

CAKE

8   medium carrots, peeled and finely grated
1½ cups unsweetened applesauce
3   cups all-purpose flour
2½ cups sugar
2   teaspoons baking powder
2   teaspoons baking soda
2   teaspoons salt
1   tablespoon ground cinnamon
1½ teaspoons ground ginger
1   cup vegetable oil
4   large eggs
2   teaspoons vanilla extract

ICING

20 ounces cream cheese, softened
1   cup unsalted butter, softened
6   cups confectioners' sugar
2   tablespoons honey
2   teaspoons grated fresh ginger

1   cup toasted pecans, chopped

Preheat oven to 350°. Spray 3 (9-inch) round cake pans with nonstick baking spray with flour. Line bottoms of pans with parchment paper; spray with nonstick baking spray with flour. Set aside.

FOR CAKE: In a medium bowl, stir together carrot and applesauce. Set aside. In a large bowl, sift together flour, sugar, baking powder, baking soda, salt, cinnamon, and ginger. Add oil, eggs, and vanilla. Beat at medium speed with an electric mixer until smooth, stopping occasionally to scrape sides of bowl. Fold in carrot mixture. Divide batter evenly among prepared pans.

Bake until a wooden pick inserted in center comes out clean, approximately 25 minutes. Let cool in pans 10 minutes. Remove from pans, and let cool completely on wire racks.

FOR ICING: In a large bowl, beat cream cheese at medium speed with an electric mixer until smooth. Add butter, beating until fluffy, approximately 2 minutes. Gradually add confectioners' sugar, honey, and ginger, beating until well combined.

Spread icing between layers and on top and sides of cake. Press pecans into sides of cake as desired.

FRESH APPLE CAKE

YIELD: 12 TO 16 SERVINGS

SWIRL

1   (8-ounce) package cream cheese, softened
½   cup confectioners' sugar
2   tablespoons all-purpose flour
1   large egg
1   tablespoon orange zest

CAKE

2   cups peeled, cored, and grated Granny Smith apple (3 apples)
2½   cups peeled, cored, and diced Granny Smith apple (3 apples)
2   teaspoons fresh lemon juice
4½   cups all-purpose flour
1¼   cups packed light brown sugar
1   cup sugar
3   teaspoons ground cinnamon
1½   teaspoons baking soda
1½   teaspoons kosher salt
1½   teaspoons ground ginger
5   large eggs, lightly beaten
1¾   cups canola oil
1½   teaspoons vanilla extract

GLAZE

1½   cups sugar
½   cup water
½   teaspoon fresh lemon juice
¾   cup heavy whipping cream
¼   cup unsalted butter, softened
1   cup confectioners' sugar, sifted

Preheat oven to 325°. Spray a 15-cup Bundt pan with nonstick baking spray with flour. Set aside.

FOR SWIRL: In a small bowl, stir together cream cheese, confectioners' sugar, flour, egg, and zest. Set aside.

FOR CAKE: In a medium bowl, combine apples and lemon juice. Set aside. In a large bowl, whisk together flour, sugars, cinnamon, baking soda, salt, and ginger. Make a well in center of dry ingredients. Add eggs, stirring to combine. (Mixture will be very dry.) Stir in canola oil. Fold in apples and vanilla.

Pour half of batter in prepared pan. Spoon cream cheese mixture over batter, avoiding edges of pan. Top with remaining batter. Using a knife, pull blade back and forth through batter to swirl cream cheese mixture. Smooth top with an offset spatula.

Bake until a wooden pick inserted near center comes out clean, approximately 1 hour and 15 minutes. Let cool on a wire rack 20 minutes. Remove from pan, and let cool completely.

FOR GLAZE: In a medium saucepan, bring sugar, ½ cup water, and lemon juice to a boil over medium-high heat. Cook, without stirring, until mixture turns light amber in color and a candy thermometer reads 340°, 10 to 15 minutes. Remove from heat, and carefully whisk in cream and butter. (Mixture will boil vigorously.) Let cool completely. Add confectioners' sugar, whisking until smooth. Drizzle over cooled cake.

BLUEBERRY SKILLET CAKE

YIELD: 6 TO 8 SERVINGS

1¼ cups all-purpose flour

¾ cup plus 1 tablespoon sugar, divided

⅓ cup plain yellow cornmeal

1½ teaspoons kosher salt

1 teaspoon baking powder

½ teaspoon baking soda

½ teaspoon lemon zest

9 tablespoons unsalted butter, divided

1 cup sour cream

2 large eggs

1 teaspoon vanilla extract

2 cups fresh blueberries, divided

Preheat oven to 350°. Place a 10-inch cast-iron skillet in oven.

In a large bowl, stir together flour, ¾ cup sugar, cornmeal, salt, baking powder, baking soda, and zest. Set aside.

In a medium microwave-safe bowl, add 8 tablespoons butter. Microwave on high in 30-second intervals until melted. Stir in sour cream, eggs, and vanilla. Make a well in center of dry ingredients. Add butter mixture, stirring to combine. Carefully remove hot skillet from oven. Melt remaining 1 tablespoon butter in skillet. Add half of batter to pan, spreading in an even layer. Sprinkle 1 cup blueberries evenly over batter. Drop spoonfuls of remaining batter over blueberries. Sprinkle with remaining 1 cup blueberries and remaining 1 tablespoon sugar.

Bake until a wooden pick inserted in center comes out clean, 35 to 40 minutes. Let cool on a wire rack 30 minutes.

RED VELVET CAKE

YIELD: 1 (9-INCH) 3-LAYER CAKE

CAKE

- 1½ cups unsalted butter, softened
- 1 cup sugar
- 1 cup firmly packed light brown sugar
- 2 large eggs
- 2½ cups all-purpose flour
- ⅓ cup natural unsweetened cocoa powder
- 1 teaspoon baking soda
- 1 teaspoon kosher salt
- 1 cup whole buttermilk
- 1 (1-ounce) bottle red food coloring
- 1 tablespoon distilled white vinegar
- 1 teaspoon vanilla extract

FROSTING

- 2 (8-ounce) packages cream cheese, softened
- 1 cup unsalted butter, softened
- 1 teaspoon vanilla extract
- 8 cups confectioners' sugar

Preheat oven to 350°. Spray 3 (9-inch) round cake pans with nonstick baking spray with flour. Line bottoms of pans with parchment paper; spray with nonstick baking spray with flour. Set aside.

FOR CAKE: In a large bowl, beat butter and sugars at medium speed with an electric mixer until fluffy, stopping occasionally to scrape sides of bowl. Add eggs, one at a time, beating well after each addition.

In a medium bowl, whisk together flour, cocoa, baking soda, and salt. With mixer on low speed, add flour mixture to butter mixture in thirds, alternating with buttermilk, beginning and ending with flour mixture. Stir in food coloring, vinegar, and vanilla. Beat until well combined. Divide batter evenly among prepared pans.

Bake until a wooden pick inserted in center comes out clean, approximately 25 minutes. Let cool in pans 10 minutes. Remove from pans, and let cool completely on wire racks.

FOR FROSTING: In a large bowl, beat cream cheese, butter, and vanilla at medium speed with an electric mixer until creamy. Gradually add confectioners' sugar, beating until smooth. Spread frosting between layers and on top and sides of cake. Cover, and refrigerate up to 2 days.

COCONUT SHEET CAKE

YIELD: APPROXIMATELY 12 SERVINGS

CAKE

- 3 cups cake flour
- 1 teaspoon baking powder
- 1 teaspoon baking soda
- ½ teaspoon salt
- 1 cup unsalted butter, softened
- 1½ cups sugar
- 4 large eggs, separated
- 1 teaspoon vanilla extract
- 1 teaspoon coconut extract
- 1¼ cups coconut milk

FROSTING

- ¾ cup unsalted butter, softened
- 4 to 5 tablespoons coconut milk
- 1 teaspoon coconut extract
- 7 cups confectioners' sugar

- 1 cup sweetened flaked coconut, toasted

Preheat oven to 350°. Spray a 13x9-inch baking dish with nonstick cooking spray. Set aside.

FOR CAKE: In a medium bowl, combine flour, baking powder, baking soda, and salt; sift twice. Set aside.

In a large bowl, beat butter and sugar at medium speed with an electric mixer until fluffy, stopping occasionally to scrape sides of bowl. Add egg yolks, one at a time, beating well after each addition. Add extracts, beating to combine. With mixer on low speed, add flour mixture to butter mixture in thirds, alternating with coconut milk, beginning and ending with flour mixture. Beat until combined.

In a medium bowl, using clean beaters, beat egg whites at high speed with an electric mixer just until stiff peaks form. Fold egg whites into batter. Gently spread into prepared dish.

Bake until a wooden pick inserted in center comes out clean, 25 to 30 minutes. Let cool completely on a wire rack.

FOR FROSTING: In a large bowl, beat butter, 4 tablespoons coconut milk, and extract at medium speed with an electric mixer until creamy. Gradually add confectioners' sugar, beating until smooth. Add remaining 1 tablespoon coconut milk to achieve a spreadable consistency, if needed. Spread frosting on cake; sprinkle with coconut.

MAYA'S FRUIT CAKE

YIELD: 10 TO 12 SERVINGS

CAKE

- 1 cup unsalted butter, softened
- 2 cups sugar
- 4 large eggs
- 3 cups all-purpose flour, divided
- 2 teaspoons baking soda
- 2 teaspoons kosher salt
- 2 teaspoons ground cinnamon
- 1 teaspoon ground cloves
- 3 cups chopped walnuts
- 2 cups mixed candied fruit
- 2 cups chopped pecans
- 1 cup dried currants
- 1 cup raisins
- 2 cups unsweetened applesauce, warmed
- ¾ cup brandy

GLAZE

- ¾ cup sugar
- ¼ cup water
- ¼ teaspoon fresh lemon juice
- ¼ cup heavy whipping cream, at room temperature
- 2 tablespoons unsalted butter, softened
- 2 tablespoons brandy
- ½ cup confectioners' sugar, sifted

Preheat oven to 300°. Spray a 15-cup Bundt pan with nonstick baking spray with flour. Set aside.

FOR CAKE: In a large bowl, beat butter and sugar at medium speed with an electric mixer until fluffy, stopping occasionally to scrape sides of bowl. Add eggs, one at a time, beating well after each addition.

In a medium bowl, combine 2 cups flour, baking soda, salt, cinnamon, and cloves. Gradually add flour mixture to butter mixture, beating until combined.

In a large bowl, combine walnuts, candied fruit, pecans, currants, raisins, and remaining 1 cup flour, stirring to coat. Add fruit and nut mixture, applesauce, and brandy to batter, stirring until combined. Pour batter in prepared pan.

Bake until a wooden pick inserted near center comes out clean, approximately 1 hour and 15 minutes. Let cool in pan 20 minutes. Invert onto a wire rack, and let cool completely.

FOR GLAZE: In a medium saucepan, bring sugar, ¼ cup water, and lemon juice to a boil over medium-high heat. Cook, without stirring, until mixture turns amber in color and a candy thermometer reads 340°, 10 to 15 minutes. Remove from heat.

Carefully whisk in cream, butter, and brandy. (Mixture will boil vigorously.) Let cool 10 minutes. Whisk in confectioners' sugar until smooth. Drizzle over cooled cake.

ULTIMATE SOUTHERN CUPCAKES

YIELD: 2 DOZEN CUPCAKES

CUPCAKES

1	cup butter, softened
1¼	cups sugar
3	large eggs
⅓	cup whole milk
⅓	cup bourbon
2	teaspoons vanilla extract
2⅓	cups self-rising flour

GLAZE

1½	cups confectioners' sugar, sifted
4	to 5 tablespoons maple syrup
¾	teaspoon fresh lemon juice
3	slices bacon, cooked and crumbled

Preheat oven to 350°. Line 24 muffin cups with paper liners. Lightly spray liners with nonstick cooking spray. Set aside.

FOR CUPCAKES: In a large bowl, beat butter and sugar at medium speed with an electric mixer until fluffy, approximately 5 minutes, stopping occasionally to scrape sides of bowl. Add eggs, one at a time, beating well after each addition. In a small bowl, combine milk, bourbon, and vanilla. With mixer on low speed, add flour to butter mixture in thirds, alternating with milk mixture, beginning and ending with flour. Beat until combined. Divide batter evenly among prepared muffin cups.

Bake until a wooden pick inserted in center comes out clean, 18 to 20 minutes. Let cool in pans 5 minutes. Remove from pans, and let cool completely on wire racks.

FOR GLAZE: In a medium bowl, whisk together confectioners' sugar, 4 tablespoons syrup, and lemon juice until smooth. Add remaining 1 tablespoon syrup, if needed. Spread glaze over cupcakes. Top with bacon.

ITALIAN CREAM CAKE

YIELD: 1 (9-INCH) 3-LAYER CAKE

CAKE

- 1½ cups butter, softened
- 2 cups sugar
- 6 large eggs, separated
- 2¼ cups all-purpose flour
- 1 teaspoon baking soda
- ½ teaspoon salt
- 1 cup sour cream
- 3 tablespoons whole milk
- 1 teaspoon vanilla extract
- 1 cup toasted pecans, chopped
- 1 cup sweetened flaked coconut
- 1 tablespoon lemon zest

FROSTING

- 1 (8-ounce) package cream cheese, softened
- ½ cup butter, softened
- 1 tablespoon lemon zest
- 2 tablespoons fresh lemon juice
- 1 teaspoon vanilla extract
- 9 cups confectioners' sugar, sifted
- 3 tablespoons whole milk

Garnish: sweetened flaked coconut, chopped toasted pecans

Preheat oven to 350°. Spray 3 (9-inch) round cake pans with nonstick baking spray with flour. Line bottoms of pans with parchment paper; spray with nonstick baking spray with flour. Set aside.

FOR CAKE: In a large bowl, beat butter and sugar at medium speed with an electric mixer until fluffy, stopping occasionally to scrape sides of bowl. Add egg yolks, one at a time, beating well after each addition.

In a medium bowl, whisk together flour, baking soda, and salt. In a small bowl, combine sour cream, milk, and vanilla. With mixer on low speed, add flour mixture to butter mixture in thirds, alternating with sour cream mixture, beginning and ending with flour mixture. Add pecans, coconut, and zest, beating until combined.

In another large bowl, using clean beaters, beat egg whites at high speed until stiff peaks form. Stir one-fourth of egg whites into batter. Gently fold in remaining egg whites. Divide batter evenly among prepared pans, gently smoothing tops with an offset spatula.

Bake until a wooden pick inserted in center comes out clean, approximately 20 minutes. Let cool in pans 10 minutes. Remove from pans, and let cool completely on wire racks.

FOR FROSTING: In a large bowl, beat cream cheese, butter, lemon zest and juice, and vanilla at medium speed with an electric mixer until creamy. Gradually beat in confectioners' sugar, adding milk, 1 tablespoon at a time, until frosting reaches a spreadable consistency.

Spread frosting between layers and on top and sides of cake. Press coconut into sides of cake, and top with pecans, if desired.

PEAR UPSIDE DOWN CAKE

YIELD: 6 TO 8 SERVINGS

1½ cups self-rising flour

1 cup sugar

¼ teaspoon ground nutmeg

3 large eggs

½ cup whole buttermilk

½ teaspoon vanilla extract

¾ cup unsalted butter, softened and divided

1 cup firmly packed light brown sugar

1½ fresh Bartlett pears, halved and cut into ¼-inch-thick slices

Preheat oven to 350°. Spray a 9-inch round cake pan with nonstick baking spray with flour. Set aside.

In a large bowl, whisk together flour, sugar, and nutmeg. Add eggs, buttermilk, and vanilla. Beat at medium-low speed with an electric mixer until smooth. Add ½ cup butter, beating to combine. Set aside.

Place remaining ¼ cup butter in prepared pan. Place pan in oven until butter melts, 2 to 3 minutes. Sprinkle brown sugar evenly over melted butter. Top with pears, arranging as desired in a single layer. Spoon batter over pears, smoothing top with an offset spatula.

Bake until a wooden pick inserted in center comes out clean, 35 to 40 minutes. Run a knife around edge of cake to loosen. Invert cake onto a serving plate, and gently remove pan.

CARAMEL CAKE

YIELD: 1 (9-INCH) 3-LAYER CAKE

CAKE

4½	cups all-purpose flour
2¼	cups sugar
1½	tablespoons baking powder
1½	teaspoons salt
1	cup plus 2 tablespoons butter, diced and softened
2¼	cups whole milk
1½	teaspoons vanilla extract
9	large egg yolks

FROSTING

1	cup sour cream
1	cup cold butter, diced
2	cups firmly packed dark brown sugar
1	teaspoon salt
5	cups confectioners' sugar, sifted
1	teaspoon vanilla extract

Preheat oven to 350°. Spray 3 (9-inch) round cake pans with nonstick baking spray with flour. Line bottoms of pans with parchment paper; spray with nonstick baking spray with flour. Set aside.

FOR CAKE: In a large bowl, stir together flour, sugar, baking powder, and salt. Add butter, milk, and vanilla. Beat at low speed with an electric mixer until combined. Increase speed to high; beat 2 minutes, stopping occasionally to scrape sides of bowl. With mixer on medium speed, add egg yolks, one at a time, beating well after each addition. Divide batter evenly among prepared pans.

Bake until a wooden pick inserted in center comes out clean, approximately 25 minutes. Let cool in pans 10 minutes. Remove from pans, and let cool completely on wire racks.

FOR FROSTING: Let sour cream stand at room temperature 30 minutes. In a large heavy saucepan, bring butter, brown sugar, and salt to a boil over medium heat, stirring constantly. Remove from heat; slowly stir in sour cream. Bring mixture just to a boil over medium heat, stirring constantly. Remove from heat. Gradually add confectioners' sugar and vanilla, beating at medium speed with an electric mixer until smooth. Let stand until mixture begins to thicken, approximately 20 minutes, stirring occasionally.

Trim tops of layers to flatten, if necessary; gently dust off crumbs. On a cake plate, place 1 cake layer; top with approximately ¾ cup frosting. Using an offset spatula, gently spread frosting back and forth, maintaining a ½-inch border, until frosting thickens, 1 to 2 minutes. Repeat procedure twice.

Secure center of cake with 2 wooden picks, spaced 3 inches apart. Spread a thin layer of frosting around sides of cake; let stand until set, approximately 20 minutes. Frost top and sides of cake with desired amount of remaining frosting. (Reheat frosting gently as needed to return to a spreadable consistency.) Remove wooden picks just before serving.

GOO GOO CLUSTER CUPCAKES

YIELD: 1 DOZEN CUPCAKES

½ cup butter, cut into small pieces

3 ounces semisweet chocolate, chopped

1¼ cups plus ½ teaspoon self-rising flour, divided

¾ cup sugar

⅛ teaspoon salt

3 large eggs

½ teaspoon vanilla extract

1 Original Goo Goo Cluster, finely chopped

1 Original Goo Goo Cluster, cut into 12 pieces

Preheat oven to 350°. Spray 12 muffin cups with nonstick baking spray with flour. Set aside.

In a small saucepan, combine butter and chocolate. Cook over medium-low heat, stirring occasionally, until smooth. Remove from heat; let cool slightly.

In a medium bowl, combine 1¼ cups flour, sugar, and salt. Add chocolate mixture, eggs, and vanilla. Beat at low speed with an electric mixer just until combined.

In a small bowl, toss finely chopped Goo Goo Cluster with remaining ½ teaspoon flour; fold into chocolate mixture. Spoon into prepared muffin cups.

Bake until tops of cupcakes spring back when lightly touched, approximately 18 minutes. Run a knife around edges to loosen.

While cupcakes are still warm, make a shallow cut in the top of each cupcake; insert 1 piece of chopped Goo Goo Cluster into each cut. Let cool 15 minutes.

PINEAPPLE CRUMB CAKE

YIELD: 6 TO 8 SERVINGS

TOPPING

⅓   cup all-purpose flour
¼   cup firmly packed dark brown
    sugar
2   tablespoons butter, softened
⅛   teaspoon salt

CAKE

2   teaspoons canola oil
8   (½-inch-thick) fresh
    pineapple rings
1½ cups all-purpose flour
¾   cup sugar
¾   teaspoon baking powder
¼   teaspoon salt
¾   cup whole milk
6   tablespoons butter, softened
½   teaspoon vanilla extract
3   large egg yolks

GLAZE

¼   cup firmly packed dark
    brown sugar
1   tablespoon dark corn syrup
1   tablespoon butter
1   tablespoon fresh lemon juice
⅛   teaspoon salt

Preheat oven to 350°.

FOR TOPPING: In a medium bowl, add flour, brown sugar, butter, and salt. Combine with fingertips until crumbly. Cover, and refrigerate until ready to use.

FOR CAKE: In a 10-inch cast-iron skillet, heat canola oil over medium-high heat. Add half of pineapple; cook 1 minute on each side or until lightly browned (reduce heat to medium, if necessary). Remove from skillet. Repeat procedure with remaining pineapple. Remove skillet from heat. Let cool approximately 20 minutes. Wipe skillet clean, and let cool.

In a medium bowl, combine flour, sugar, baking powder, and salt. Add milk, butter, and vanilla. Beat at low speed with an electric mixer until combined, approximately 1 minute. Beat at high speed 2 minutes, stopping occasionally to scrape sides of bowl. With mixer on low speed, add egg yolks, one at a time, beating well after each addition. Spread batter in skillet. Arrange pineapple over batter, overlapping slices. Sprinkle with topping.

Bake until golden brown, approximately 35 minutes. Let cool 30 minutes.

FOR GLAZE: In a small saucepan, combine brown sugar, syrup, butter, lemon juice, and salt. Bring to a simmer over medium heat, stirring frequently. Cook until smooth, approximately 1 minute. Remove from heat. Drizzle over cake.

LEMONADE POUND CAKE

YIELD: APPROXIMATELY 12 SERVINGS

1½ cups unsalted butter, softened

2 cups sugar

5 large eggs

3 cups all-purpose flour

1 teaspoon baking soda

1 teaspoon salt

¾ cup frozen lemonade concentrate, thawed

½ cup sour cream

1 tablespoon lemon zest

GLAZE

⅓ cup frozen lemonade concentrate, thawed

½ teaspoon lemon zest

2 cups confectioners' sugar

Preheat oven to 325°. Spray a 15-cup Bundt pan with nonstick baking spray with flour. Set aside.

FOR CAKE: In a large bowl, beat butter and sugar at medium speed with an electric mixer until fluffy, stopping occasionally to scrape sides of bowl. Add eggs, one at a time, beating well after each addition.

In a medium bowl, stir together flour, baking soda, and salt. With mixer on low speed, add flour mixture to butter mixture in thirds, alternating with lemonade and sour cream, beginning and ending with flour mixture. Add zest, beating to combine. Pour batter into prepared pan.

Bake until a wooden pick inserted near center comes out clean, approximately 1 hour. Let cool in pan 10 minutes. Invert onto a wire rack, and let cool slightly.

FOR GLAZE: In a medium bowl, combine lemonade and zest. Gradually whisk in confectioners' sugar until smooth. Drizzle glaze over warm cake.

PIES, PUDDINGS, and COBBLERS

DOUBLE APPLE-CRANBERRY PIE

YIELD: 1 (9-INCH) DEEP-DISH PIE

3   **large Granny Smith apples, peeled, cored, and sliced**

3   **large Braeburn apples, peeled, cored, and sliced**

½   **cup sweetened dried cranberries**

1   **tablespoon fresh lemon juice**

½   **cup plus 2 teaspoons sugar, divided**

½   **cup firmly packed light brown sugar**

¼   **cup all-purpose flour**

1   **teaspoon ground cinnamon**

¼   **teaspoon ground nutmeg**

1   **(14.1-ounce) package refrigerated piecrusts (2 sheets)**

2   **tablespoons butter, cut into pieces**

1   **large egg yolk, lightly beaten**

Preheat oven to 425°.

In a large bowl, combine apples, cranberries, and lemon juice.

In a small bowl, combine ½ cup sugar, brown sugar, flour, cinnamon, and nutmeg. Pour over apples, stirring gently. Set aside.

On a lightly floured surface, roll 1 piecrust into a 10-inch circle. Transfer to a 9-inch deep-dish pie plate, pressing into bottom and up sides. Pour filling into crust. (Filling will mound above edge of pie plate.) Dot evenly with butter.

Unroll remaining piecrust; cut into 1-inch strips. Arrange strips over filling in a lattice design. Fold edges under, and crimp as desired. Brush lattice with egg yolk. Sprinkle with remaining 2 teaspoons sugar.

Bake on lowest rack 30 minutes. Lightly cover with aluminum foil, and bake until apples are soft, 30 to 45 minutes more. Let cool completely on a wire rack.

FROZEN PEPPERMINT MOUSSE PIE

YIELD: 1 (9-INCH) PIE

CRUST

1²/₃	cups finely ground chocolate wafers (about 24 wafers)
¼	cup sugar
¼	cup butter, melted

FILLING

1	tablespoon all-purpose flour
⅛	teaspoon salt
1	cup whole milk
1	large egg yolk
¼	cup cream cheese, cut into pieces and softened
2	(1-ounce) squares white chocolate, finely chopped
2	tablespoons peppermint liqueur, such as white crème de menthe
1	to 2 drops red food coloring (optional)
1	cup heavy whipping cream
¼	cup confectioners' sugar

Garnish: sweetened whipped cream, crushed peppermints

Spray a 9-inch pie plate with nonstick cooking spray. Set aside.

FOR CRUST: In a medium bowl, stir together ground wafers, sugar, and melted butter until moistened. Using the bottom of a measuring cup, press mixture into bottom and up sides of prepared pie plate. Place in freezer while preparing filling.

FOR FILLING: In a medium saucepan, combine flour and salt; whisk in milk. Bring to a boil over medium heat, stirring constantly. Cook, stirring constantly, until thickened and bubbly, approximately 2 minutes. Remove from heat. Place egg yolk in a medium bowl. Gradually add half of hot milk mixture, whisking to combine. Whisk egg mixture into remaining hot milk mixture in saucepan. Cook over medium-low heat, stirring constantly, until thickened and bubbly, approximately 2 minutes. Remove from heat. Add cream cheese and white chocolate; stir until melted and smooth. Stir in liqueur and food coloring, if using. Transfer mixture to a bowl. Cover, and refrigerate until chilled, approximately 1 hour.

In a medium bowl, combine cream and confectioners' sugar. Beat at high speed with an electric mixer until stiff peaks form. Gently fold into cream cheese mixture. Spread evenly in prepared crust. Freeze until firm, 4 to 5 hours. Remove from freezer 10 minutes before serving. Garnish with whipped cream and crushed peppermints, if desired.

EASY PEACH COBBLER

YIELD: APPROXIMATELY 8 SERVINGS

½ cup butter
1 cup all-purpose flour
1 cup sugar
1 tablespoon baking powder
1 cup whole buttermilk
1 cup firmly packed light brown
   sugar
1½ tablespoons cornstarch
½ teaspoon ground cinnamon
½ teaspoon salt
¼ teaspoon ground nutmeg
5 cups peeled, pitted, and sliced
   fresh peaches
1 tablespoon vanilla extract
Vanilla ice cream (optional)

Preheat oven to 375°.

In a 2-quart baking dish, place butter. Place dish in oven until butter melts, approximately 5 minutes.

In a medium bowl, combine flour, sugar, and baking powder. Add buttermilk, whisking until smooth. Pour buttermilk mixture over melted butter in prepared dish. (Do not stir.) Set aside.

In a medium saucepan, whisk together brown sugar, cornstarch, cinnamon, salt, and nutmeg. Add peaches and vanilla, stirring to combine. Cook over medium-high heat, stirring often, until mixture comes to a boil. Remove from heat. Pour peach mixture over batter.

Bake until browned and bubbly, approximately 45 minutes. Let cool slightly. Serve warm with vanilla ice cream, if desired.

FROZEN KEY LIME PIE

CRUST

2   cups finely ground gingersnap
     crumbs
½   cup sugar
½   cup butter, melted

FILLING

1   cup cream of coconut
¼   cup lime zest
½   cup fresh Key lime juice
1   (8-ounce) package cream cheese,
     softened
1   cup confectioners' sugar
1   (8-ounce) container vanilla-
     flavored Greek yogurt
1   (8-ounce) container frozen
     nondairy whipped topping,
     thawed

Garnish: lime zest

FOR CRUST: In a large bowl, stir together gingersnap crumbs, sugar, and melted butter until moistened. Using the bottom of a measuring cup, press mixture into bottom and up sides of a 10-inch deep-dish pie plate. Place in freezer while preparing filling.

FOR FILLING: In a medium bowl, whisk together cream of coconut and lime zest and juice.

In a large bowl, beat cream cheese at high speed with an electric mixer until smooth, approximately 3 minutes. Add confectioners' sugar and yogurt, beating until smooth. Add coconut mixture, beating to combine. Add whipped topping, beating until smooth.

Spoon mixture into prepared crust, smoothing top with an offset spatula. Freeze 4 hours or up to one week. Garnish with lime zest, if desired.

BANANA PUDDING TART

YIELD: 1 (9½-INCH) TART

CRUST

2½ cups vanilla wafer crumbs
½ cup butter, melted
2 tablespoons firmly packed light brown sugar
1 large egg white, lightly beaten

FILLING

4 large egg yolks
¾ cup firmly packed light brown sugar
2 cups heavy whipping cream
½ cup fresh banana purée
1 teaspoon vanilla extract
½ vanilla bean, split lengthwise and seeds scraped and reserved
⅛ teaspoon sea salt
7 tablespoons butter, softened

TOPPING

4 tablespoons sugar, divided
1 banana, sliced

Preheat oven to 350°.

FOR CRUST: In a medium bowl, stir together crumbs, melted butter, and brown sugar. Using the bottom of a measuring cup, press into bottom and up sides of a 9½-inch removable-bottom tart pan. Brush bottom of crust with egg white. Bake until golden brown, 8 to 10 minutes. Let cool on a wire rack.

Reduce oven to 275°.

FOR FILLING: In a large bowl, beat egg yolks and brown sugar at high speed with an electric mixer until thick and smooth.

In a medium saucepan, combine cream, banana purée, extract, vanilla bean and reserved seeds, and salt. Cook over medium heat, whisking often, just until mixture begins to boil. Remove from heat. Add butter, whisking until melted and combined. Gradually add 1 cup hot cream mixture to egg yolk mixture, whisking constantly. Add egg mixture to cream mixture, whisking to combine. Strain mixture through a fine-mesh sieve into prepared crust. Smooth top with an offset spatula. Bake until set, approximately 55 minutes. Let cool to room temperature. Refrigerate at least 4 hours.

FOR TOPPING: Sprinkle 3 tablespoons sugar evenly over filling. Holding a kitchen torch at least 6 inches away from surface of tart, carefully caramelize sugar. Let stand 2 minutes.

Place banana slices on a baking sheet, and sprinkle with remaining 1 tablespoon sugar. Caramelize with torch. Garnish tart with banana. Serve immediately.

PINEAPPLE COBBLER

YIELD: APPROXIMATELY 8 SERVINGS

5   cups cubed fresh pineapple

8   tablespoons butter, melted and
     divided

¼   cup sugar

2   tablespoons all-purpose flour

1   tablespoon lime zest

1   tablespoon fresh lime juice

1½   cups old-fashioned oats

1¼   cups sweetened flaked coconut

½   cup chopped macadamia nuts

½   teaspoon salt

Coconut ice cream or gelato (optional)

Preheat oven to 425°.

In a large bowl, combine pineapple, 2 tablespoons melted butter, sugar, flour, and lime zest and juice, stirring gently to combine. Spoon into an 8x8-inch baking pan.

In a medium bowl, stir together oats, coconut, macadamias, salt, and remaining 6 tablespoons melted butter. Spoon over pineapple mixture.

Bake until golden brown and bubbly, 20 to 30 minutes. Serve with ice cream or gelato, if desired.

CHOCOLATE AND PISTACHIO CREAM PIE

YIELD: 1 (9-INCH) PIE

CRUST
24	chocolate wafers
1/3	cup roasted salted pistachios, shelled
3	tablespoons sugar
3	tablespoons butter, softened

FILLING
3/4	cup sugar
2 1/2	tablespoons natural unsweetened cocoa powder
1 1/2	tablespoons cornstarch
1/8	teaspoon salt
1 1/2	cups half-and-half
3	large egg yolks
3/4	cup finely chopped bittersweet chocolate
3	tablespoons butter
1	teaspoon vanilla extract

Garnish: 2/3 cup chopped roasted salted pistachios

Preheat oven to 375°. Spray a 9-inch pie plate with nonstick cooking spray. Set aside.

FOR CRUST: In the work bowl of a food processor, combine wafers and pistachios. Pulse until finely ground, approximately 10 times. Add sugar and butter; pulse until combined, 4 or 5 times. Using the bottom of a measuring cup, press mixture into bottom and up sides of prepared pie plate.

Bake 9 to 11 minutes. Let cool completely on a wire rack.

FOR FILLING: In a medium saucepan, combine sugar, cocoa, cornstarch, and salt. Add half-and-half and egg yolks, whisking until smooth. Bring to a boil over medium-high heat, stirring constantly. Reduce heat to medium. Cook, stirring constantly, until thickened and bubbly, approximately 2 minutes. Remove from heat.

Add chocolate, butter, and vanilla, stirring until melted. Pour mixture into prepared crust. Let cool 10 minutes on a wire rack.

Place a piece of plastic wrap directly on surface of filling. Refrigerate until firm, approximately 4 hours. Remove plastic wrap, and smooth surface of pie with an offset spatula. Garnish with pistachios, if desired.

LEMON-RICOTTA PIE

YIELD: 1 (9-INCH) PIE

CRUST

2	cups all-purpose flour
¼	cup sugar
½	teaspoon ground cinnamon
⅜	teaspoon ground ginger
¼	teaspoon ground allspice
¼	teaspoon kosher salt
⅛	teaspoon ground nutmeg
6	tablespoons cold unsalted butter, cut into pieces
6	tablespoons ice water

FILLING

2	cups whole-milk ricotta cheese
½	cup sour cream
⅓	cup superfine sugar
2	large eggs
2	teaspoons lemon zest
2	tablespoons fresh lemon juice
¼	teaspoon kosher salt

FOR CRUST: In the work bowl of a food processor, pulse together flour, sugar, cinnamon, ginger, allspice, salt, and nutmeg. Add butter, pulsing until crumbly, approximately 1 minute.

With food processor running, add 6 tablespoons ice water in a slow steady stream until a dough forms. Shape dough into a disk, and cover with plastic wrap. Refrigerate until firm, approximately 2 hours.

Preheat oven to 350°.

On a lightly floured surface, roll dough into a 12-inch circle, approximately ⅛ inch thick. Transfer to a 9-inch pie plate, pressing into bottom and up sides. Trim even with edge of dish. Cut ½-inch notches in piecrust edge, spacing ½ inch apart. Cover with plastic wrap, and refrigerate 30 minutes.

Prick bottom and sides of dough with a fork 10 times. Top with a piece of parchment paper, letting ends extend over edges of plate. Add pie weights. Bake until edges are lightly browned, 12 to 16 minutes. Carefully remove paper and weights. Let cool on a wire rack.

FOR FILLING: In the work bowl of a food processor, combine ricotta, sour cream, sugar, eggs, lemon zest and juice, and salt. Process until smooth, approximately 3 minutes. Pour batter into prepared crust. Place on a rimmed baking sheet.

Bake until filling is set and just begins to brown, 30 to 35 minutes. Transfer to a wire rack, and let cool completely.

BLACK BOTTOM BANANA CREAM PIE

YIELD: 1 (9-INCH) PIE

CRUST

2 cups chocolate graham cracker crumbs

½ cup sugar

½ cup butter, melted

FILLING

5 ounces semisweet baking chocolate, chopped

⅓ cup heavy whipping cream

2 tablespoons butter

1½ cups half-and-half

1 teaspoon vanilla extract

½ cup sugar

2 tablespoons cornstarch

2 large eggs

1 large egg yolk

3 to 4 ripe bananas

1 (12-ounce) container frozen nondairy whipped topping, thawed

FOR CRUST: In a medium bowl, stir together graham cracker crumbs, sugar, and melted butter. Using the bottom of a measuring cup, press mixture into bottom and up sides of a 9-inch pie plate. Refrigerate at least 15 minutes.

FOR FILLING: In a medium bowl, place chopped chocolate. Set aside.

In a small saucepan, bring cream and butter to a boil over medium-high heat. Remove from heat, and pour over chopped chocolate. Whisk until smooth.

Pour chocolate mixture in prepared crust. Refrigerate at least 30 minutes.

In a medium saucepan, combine half-and-half and vanilla. Cook over medium heat, stirring often, until mixture begins to simmer, 3 to 5 minutes.

In a medium bowl, whisk together sugar and cornstarch. Add eggs and egg yolk, whisking until smooth. Gradually add half-and-half mixture to egg mixture, whisking well. Transfer mixture to saucepan. Cook over medium heat, stirring constantly, until mixture comes to a boil and thickens, approximately 6 minutes. Boil 1 minute. Strain through a fine-mesh sieve into a medium bowl. Refrigerate 20 minutes.

Slice bananas ¼ inch thick; arrange over chocolate layer in prepared crust. Gently spread custard mixture over bananas. Refrigerate 2 to 4 hours.

Spread with whipped topping. Cover, and refrigerate up to 3 days.

SWEET POTATO-PECAN PIE

YIELD: 1 (9-INCH) DEEP-DISH PIE

CRUST AND FILLING

½	(14.1-ounce) package refrigerated piecrusts (1 sheet)
2	cups cooked mashed sweet potato (about 2 large)
⅓	cup firmly packed light brown sugar
2	large eggs, lightly beaten
2	tablespoons unsalted butter, melted
2	tablespoons unsulphured molasses
1	tablespoon all-purpose flour
1	teaspoon vanilla extract
¾	teaspoon kosher salt
½	teaspoon ground cinnamon
½	teaspoon orange zest
1	cup evaporated milk

TOPPING

1½	cups firmly packed light brown sugar
6	tablespoons unsalted butter, melted
4	tablespoons unsulphured molasses
2	tablespoons heavy whipping cream
2	teaspoons vanilla extract
2	cups toasted pecans, chopped
¼	teaspoon kosher salt

Preheat oven to 350°.

FOR CRUST AND FILLING: On a lightly floured surface, roll piecrust into a 12-inch circle. Transfer to a 9-inch deep-dish pie plate, pressing into bottom and up sides. Fold edges under, and crimp as desired. Prick bottom and sides 10 times with a fork. Top with a piece of parchment paper, letting ends extend over edges of plate. Fill with pie weights.

Bake until lightly browned, approximately 15 minutes. Carefully remove paper and weights. Let cool completely.

In a large bowl, whisk together sweet potato, brown sugar, eggs, melted butter, molasses, flour, vanilla, salt, cinnamon, and zest. Slowly stir in evaporated milk. Pour mixture into cooled crust.

Bake just until center is set, 30 to 40 minutes. (Cover with aluminum foil to prevent excess browning, if necessary.) Let cool on a wire rack.

FOR TOPPING: In a small saucepan, cook brown sugar, melted butter, and molasses over medium heat, stirring until sugar dissolves and mixture just begins to boil. Add cream and vanilla, stirring constantly until combined. Stir in pecans and salt. Bring to a boil, stirring constantly. Remove from heat. Pour topping over pie, spreading to seal edges. Refrigerate at least 4 hours before serving.

BUTTERMILK CHESS PIE

YIELD: 1 (9-INCH) PIE

2   cups all-purpose flour
½   cup sugar
½   teaspoon salt
5   tablespoons cold butter, diced
⅓   cup plus 1 tablespoon ice water

FILLING

1   cup sugar
3   tablespoons all-purpose flour
1½   tablespoons plain yellow
     cornmeal
½   teaspoon salt
5   large eggs, at room temperature
¾   cup whole buttermilk, at room
     temperature
3   tablespoons plain Greek yogurt
1   tablespoon fresh lemon juice
⅓   cup butter, melted and cooled
2   teaspoons vanilla extract

Preheat oven to 350°.

FOR CRUST: In the work bowl of a food processor, pulse together flour, sugar, and salt. Add butter, pulsing until mixture resembles coarse crumbs.

With processor running, add ⅓ cup plus 1 tablespoon ice water in a slow steady stream until a dough forms. Turn out dough; shape into a disk. Cover with plastic wrap, and refrigerate at least 2 hours. Remove from refrigerator 20 minutes before rolling.

On a lightly floured surface, roll dough into a 12-inch circle. Transfer to a 9-inch pie plate, pressing into bottom and up sides. Fold edges under, and crimp as desired. Set aside.

FOR FILLING: In a medium bowl, whisk together sugar, flour, cornmeal, and salt. In another medium bowl, whisk eggs until smooth. Add sugar mixture to eggs, whisking to combine.

In a small bowl, combine buttermilk, yogurt, and lemon juice, whisking until smooth. Add melted butter and vanilla. Gradually add buttermilk mixture to flour mixture, whisking after each addition until smooth. Pour into prepared crust. Bake 20 minutes. Cover loosely with aluminum foil. Bake until set and light golden brown, 20 to 25 minutes.

Let cool completely on a wire rack. Cover, and refrigerate up to 5 days.

PLUM TART

YIELD: 1 (11X8-INCH) TART

CRUST

2½ cups finely ground vanilla wafer
   crumbs
½ cup finely ground toasted walnuts
¼ cup sugar
¼ teaspoon salt
5 tablespoons unsalted butter,
   melted

FILLING

2 cups heavy whipping cream
½ cup confectioners' sugar
½ teaspoon ground cardamom
4 cups sliced fresh plums
   (7 to 8 plums)

Preheat oven to 350°.

FOR CRUST: In the work bowl of a food processor, pulse together wafer crumbs, walnuts, sugar, and salt. With processor running, gradually add melted butter. Process until well combined.

Using the bottom of a measuring cup, press mixture into bottom and up sides of an 11x8-inch removable-bottom tart pan.

Bake until lightly browned, 15 to 20 minutes. Let cool completely.

FOR FILLING: In a large bowl, beat cream, confectioners' sugar, and cardamom at medium-high speed with an electric mixer until stiff peaks form. Spread in an even layer in prepared crust.

Arrange plums over cream as desired. Carefully remove tart from pan.

SWEET POTATO-CREAM CHEESE PIE

YIELD: 1 (9-INCH) PIE

CRUST

1½ **cups finely ground gingersnap crumbs (about 22 cookies)**
½   **cup pecan halves, toasted**
¼   **cup butter, melted**

FILLING

2   **cups peeled and chopped sweet potato**
5   **tablespoons sugar, divided**
4   **tablespoons whole milk, divided**
2   **teaspoons vanilla extract, divided**
2   **teaspoons all-purpose flour, divided**
½   **teaspoon pumpkin pie spice**
2   **large eggs, divided**
12 **ounces cream cheese, softened**

TOPPING

⅓   **cup pecan halves, toasted**
3   **tablespoons sugar**

Preheat oven to 325°. Spray a 9-inch pie plate with nonstick cooking spray. Set aside.

FOR CRUST: In the work bowl of a food processor, pulse gingersnap crumbs and pecans until finely ground. Add melted butter; pulse until combined, 3 or 4 times. Using the bottom of a measuring cup, press mixture into bottom and up sides of prepared pie plate. Set aside.

FOR FILLING: In a medium saucepan, place sweet potato. Add water to cover by 1 inch. Bring to a boil over medium-high heat. Cook until tender, 7 to 9 minutes. Drain.

In the work bowl of a food processor, combine sweet potato, 2 tablespoons sugar, 2 tablespoons milk, 1 teaspoon vanilla, 1 teaspoon flour, pumpkin pie spice, and 1 egg. Process until smooth, stopping occasionally to scrape sides of bowl. Transfer to a large bowl. In the work bowl of a food processor, combine cream cheese, remaining 3 tablespoons sugar, remaining 2 tablespoons milk, remaining 1 teaspoon vanilla, remaining 1 teaspoon flour, and remaining 1 egg. Process until smooth, stopping occasionally to scrape sides of bowl.

Spread cream cheese mixture in prepared crust. Spread sweet potato mixture over cream cheese mixture, leaving a ½-inch border around edges. Bake until set, approximately 40 minutes. Let cool 1 hour on a wire rack. Lightly cover, and refrigerate until chilled, approximately 3 hours.

FOR TOPPING: Lightly spray a sheet of aluminum foil with nonstick cooking spray. Place pecans on foil in an even layer, arranging in a 5-inch circle.

In a medium heavy skillet, place sugar in an even layer. Cook over medium heat, without stirring, until most of sugar turns golden brown, approximately 6 minutes. Gently stir until all of sugar is golden brown and smooth. Pour over pecans. Let cool until completely hardened. Break into pieces; sprinkle over pie.

COOKIES AND CREAM PIE

YIELD: 1 (9-INCH) PIE

CRUST

2¼ cups finely crushed chocolate
sandwich cookies, such as Oreos
(about 24 cookies)

¼ cup unsalted butter, melted

FILLING

1 (8-ounce) package cream cheese,
softened

1 cup marshmallow crème,
such as Marshmallow Fluff

1 cup heavy whipping cream

1⅓ cups lightly crushed chocolate
sandwich cookies (about 12
cookies)

Garnish: sweetened whipped cream,
chocolate sandwich cookie

Preheat oven to 350°.

FOR CRUST: In a medium bowl, stir together crushed cookies and melted butter until combined. Using the bottom of a measuring cup, press mixture into bottom and up sides of a 9-inch pie plate.

Bake until set, approximately 12 minutes. Let cool completely on a wire rack.

FOR FILLING: In a large bowl, beat cream cheese and marshmallow crème at medium speed with an electric mixer until smooth. In a medium bowl, beat cream until stiff peaks form, approximately 4 minutes.

Gently fold whipped cream into cream cheese mixture; stir in crushed cookies. Spread filling into cooled crust, smoothing top with an offset spatula.

Refrigerate at least 4 hours. Top with whipped cream and cookie before serving, if desired.

FRIED PEACH PIES

YIELD: APPROXIMATELY 1 DOZEN HAND PIES

DOUGH

2   cups plus 2 tablespoons
     all-purpose flour
2½   teaspoons confectioners' sugar
¾   teaspoon salt
4   tablespoons cold unsalted butter,
     diced
4   tablespoons cold lard, diced
½   cup ice water

FILLING

4   large fresh peaches, peeled,
     pitted, and finely chopped
½   cup firmly packed light brown
     sugar
2   tablespoons butter
1   teaspoon vanilla extract
⅛   teaspoon ground cinnamon
⅛   teaspoon salt
⅛   teaspoon ground nutmeg

Vegetable oil for frying
Garnish: confectioners' sugar

FOR DOUGH: In a large bowl, sift together flour, confectioners' sugar, and salt. Using a pastry blender, cut in butter and lard until mixture resembles coarse crumbs. Sprinkle ice water, 1 tablespoon at a time, over flour mixture, stirring until moistened. Gather dough into a ball. Divide dough in half; shape into 2 disks. Cover each with plastic wrap, and refrigerate at least 2 hours.

FOR FILLING: In a medium saucepan, combine peaches, brown sugar, butter, vanilla, cinnamon, salt, and nutmeg. Cook over medium heat, stirring occasionally, until peaches are tender, approximately 20 minutes. Remove from heat, and let cool completely.

On a lightly floured surface, roll 1 disk of dough ⅛ inch thick. Using a 4½-inch round cutter, cut 6 rounds, and set aside. Repeat with remaining dough, rerolling scraps only once.

Place approximately 1 tablespoon filling in center of each round. Fold in half, pressing edges together with a fork to seal. Refrigerate 1 hour.

In a large Dutch oven, fill with oil to two-thirds full. Heat over medium heat until a deep-fry thermometer reads 350°. Cook pies in batches, turning occasionally, until golden brown, 6 to 8 minutes. (Adjust heat as needed to maintain 350°.) Let drain on paper towels. Garnish with confectioners' sugar, if desired.

BLACK AND BLUE COBBLER

YIELD: APPROXIMATELY 12 SERVINGS

CRUST

½ cup butter, softened
⅓ cup sugar
1 large egg
1½ cups all-purpose flour
½ teaspoon salt

FILLING

8 cups fresh blackberries
   (approximately 2¼ pounds)
2 cups fresh blueberries
¾ cup plus 1 tablespoon sugar,
   divided
½ cup all-purpose flour
⅛ teaspoon salt
2 tablespoons fresh lemon juice
¼ teaspoon ground cinnamon
¼ cup cold butter, cut into small
   pieces

1 large egg, lightly beaten
1 teaspoon water

Garnish: 1 teaspoon sugar
Vanilla ice cream (optional)

FOR CRUST: In a large bowl, beat butter and sugar at medium speed with an electric mixer until creamy. Add egg, beating until combined. Gradually add flour and salt. Beat until smooth, stopping occasionally to scrape sides of bowl. (Mixture will be thick.)

On a lightly floured surface, place dough. Knead 3 or 4 times. Divide in half, shaping into 2 small rectangles. Cover each with plastic wrap; refrigerate 1 hour.

Preheat oven to 375°.

FOR FILLING: In a 13x9-inch baking dish, combine blackberries, blueberries, ¾ cup sugar, flour, salt, lemon juice, and cinnamon, stirring gently. Dot evenly with butter.

On a lightly floured surface, roll one portion of dough into a 13x4-inch rectangle. Cut into 4 strips. Place strips lengthwise over fruit mixture, trimming edges, if necessary. Roll remaining portion of dough into a 9x6-inch rectangle. Cut into 6 strips. Place strips crosswise over pan, trimming edges, if necessary.

In a small bowl, whisk together egg and 1 teaspoon water; lightly brush over dough. Sprinkle with remaining 1 tablespoon sugar.

Bake until crust is golden brown and filling is bubbly, approximately 45 minutes. Garnish with sugar, if desired. Let stand 20 minutes before serving. Serve with ice cream, if desired.

SWEET POTATO TARTS

YIELD: 5 (4½-INCH) TARTS OR 1 (9-INCH) TART

CRUST

1	cup chopped pecans
1	cup graham cracker crumbs
¼	cup firmly packed light brown sugar
½	teaspoon ground cinnamon
5	tablespoons butter, melted

FILLING

1	cup cooked mashed sweet potato (about 1 large potato)
2	large eggs, lightly beaten
¼	cup firmly packed light brown sugar
3	tablespoons butter, melted
3	tablespoons heavy whipping cream
1	tablespoon honey
½	teaspoon ground cinnamon
¼	teaspoon ground nutmeg
¼	teaspoon ground cloves

TOPPING

1	cup miniature marshmallows

Preheat oven to 350°.

FOR CRUST: In the work bowl of a food processor, pulse pecans, graham cracker crumbs, brown sugar, and cinnamon until crumbly. Add melted butter, pulsing just until moistened. Using the bottom of a measuring cup, press into bottom and up sides of 5 (4½-inch) removable-bottom tart pans or 1 (9-inch) removable-bottom tart pan. Place on a baking sheet.

Bake 10 minutes. Let cool.

FOR FILLING: In a large bowl, combine sweet potato, eggs, brown sugar, melted butter, cream, honey, cinnamon, nutmeg, and cloves. Beat at medium speed with an electric mixer until combined. Divide mixture evenly among cooled crusts.

Bake until set, approximately 25 minutes for individual tarts or 35 minutes for 9-inch tart. Let cool on a wire rack 15 minutes.

FOR TOPPING: Set oven to broil. Top tarts with marshmallows. Broil, 5 inches from heat, watching carefully, until lightly toasted, 1 to 2 minutes.

PEANUT BUTTER PIE

YIELD: 1 (9-INCH) PIE

CRUST

1	(5-ounce) sleeve cinnamon graham crackers (about 9 whole crackers)
1	cup roasted salted peanuts
2	tablespoons sugar
6	tablespoons butter, slightly softened

FILLING

1½	cups creamy peanut butter
1	(8-ounce) package cream cheese, softened
1	cup confectioners' sugar, sifted
2	cups heavy whipping cream

Garnish: chopped peanuts, sweetened whipped cream

Preheat oven to 350°. Lightly spray a 9-inch pie plate with nonstick cooking spray.

FOR CRUST: In the work bowl of a food processor, combine graham crackers, peanuts, and sugar. Pulse until finely ground, 5 or 6 times. Add butter; pulse until combined, 3 or 4 times. Reserve 1 tablespoon crumb mixture for garnish. Spoon remaining crumb mixture into prepared pie plate. Using the bottom of a measuring cup, press into bottom and up sides.

Bake until lightly browned, approximately 10 minutes. Let cool completely.

FOR FILLING: In a large bowl, beat peanut butter and cream cheese at medium speed with an electric mixer until smooth, stopping occasionally to scrape sides of bowl. Add confectioners' sugar, beating until combined. Add cream; beat on low speed until combined. Increase speed to high; beat just until mixture thickens. (Be careful to not overbeat.) Spread filling evenly in prepared crust. Cover, and refrigerate until firm, approximately 4 hours. Garnish with reserved crumb mixture, chopped peanuts, and whipped cream, if desired.

BLUEBERRY CRISP

YIELD: 6 TO 8 SERVINGS

6   cups fresh blueberries
    (about 2¼ pounds)
¾   cup sugar, divided
½   cup plus 3 tablespoons
    all-purpose flour, divided
2   teaspoons lemon zest
2   tablespoons fresh lemon juice
1   teaspoon ground cinnamon
¼   cup firmly packed light brown
    sugar
¼   cup old-fashioned oats
4   tablespoons butter, chilled and
    cut into ½-inch pieces
¼   teaspoon almond extract
¼   teaspoon salt
Garnish: ½ cup sliced almonds

Preheat oven to 350°.

In a medium bowl, stir together blueberries, ½ cup sugar, 3 tablespoons flour, lemon zest and juice, and cinnamon. Spoon mixture into a 3-quart baking dish, and set aside.

In the work bowl of a food processor, add remaining ¼ cup sugar, remaining ½ cup flour, brown sugar, oats, butter, extract, and salt. Pulse until mixture resembles coarse crumbs. Sprinkle mixture over blueberries.

Bake until browned and bubbly, approximately 45 minutes. Let cool slightly. Garnish with almonds, if desired.

BANANA PUDDING

YIELD: APPROXIMATELY 12 SERVINGS

8   large eggs, separated

2   cups sugar, divided

½   cup all-purpose flour

⅛   teaspoon salt

4½ cups whole milk

1   vanilla bean, split lengthwise
    and seeds scraped and reserved

1   tablespoon butter

1   (11-ounce) box vanilla wafers

6   bananas, sliced

½   teaspoon cream of tartar

Preheat oven to 375°.

In a large bowl, whisk together egg yolks and 1 cup sugar. In a large heavy saucepan, place flour and salt. Whisk in milk. Add reserved vanilla bean seeds. Bring to a simmer over medium heat, stirring constantly. Remove from heat. Gradually add half of hot milk mixture to egg yolk mixture, whisking to combine. Stir egg mixture into remaining hot milk mixture in pan. Cook, stirring constantly, over medium heat until mixture comes to a simmer. Cook, stirring constantly, until thickened and bubbly, approximately 2 minutes. Remove from heat. Add butter, stirring until melted.

In a shallow 3-quart baking dish, evenly layer half of vanilla wafers, half of banana slices, and half of vanilla pudding. Repeat layers once.

In another large bowl, using clean beaters, beat egg whites and cream of tartar at high speed with an electric mixer until foamy. Gradually add remaining 1 cup sugar, beating just until stiff peaks form. Spoon over pudding, spreading to seal edges.

Bake until lightly browned, 10 to 12 minutes. Let cool 30 minutes on a wire rack. Serve warm, or refrigerate up to 4 hours.

CHOCOLATE AND CARAMEL PIE

YIELD: 1 (9-INCH) PIE

½   (14.1-ounce) package refrigerated
    piecrusts (1 sheet)
2   (12-ounce) jars prepared caramel
    topping
2   large eggs
12 ounces bittersweet chocolate,
    chopped
1⅔ cups heavy whipping cream,
    divided
½   cup sugar, divided
1   tablespoon unsalted butter
¼   cup toffee bits

Preheat oven to 350°.

In a 9-inch pie plate, press piecrust into bottom and up sides. Fold edges under, and crimp as desired. Set aside.

In a medium bowl, whisk together caramel topping and eggs until smooth. Pour in prepared crust.

Bake until set, approximately 45 minutes. (Center will jiggle slightly.) Let cool 20 minutes. Refrigerate, uncovered, 1 hour.

Place chocolate in a medium bowl. In a medium saucepan, bring ⅓ cup cream, ¼ cup sugar, and butter to a boil over medium-high heat. Pour hot cream mixture over chocolate, whisking until smooth. Pour chocolate mixture over pie. Refrigerate, uncovered, 1 hour.

In a medium bowl, combine remaining 1⅓ cups cream and remaining ¼ cup sugar. Beat at medium-high speed with an electric mixer until medium peaks form.

Top with whipped cream; sprinkle with toffee bits. Cover, and refrigerate up to 3 days.

BREAD PUDDING

YIELD: 10 TO 12 SERVINGS

BREAD PUDDING

1	(1-pound) loaf French bread, cut into 1-inch pieces
6	cups whole milk
6	large eggs
1¼	cups sugar
¼	cup bourbon
3	tablespoons molasses
2	teaspoons vanilla extract
½	teaspoon salt
½	teaspoon ground cinnamon

SAUCE

1¼	cups firmly packed dark brown sugar
½	cup butter
⅓	cup bourbon
⅓	cup water
⅛	teaspoon salt
1	cup chopped pecans, toasted

Preheat oven to 350°. Spray a 13x9-inch baking dish with nonstick cooking spray. Set aside.

FOR BREAD PUDDING: On a large rimmed baking sheet, place bread. Bake until dry, approximately 15 minutes. Let cool.

In a large bowl, whisk together milk, eggs, sugar, bourbon, molasses, vanilla, salt, and cinnamon. Add bread, stirring to combine. Pour bread mixture into prepared dish. Using a spatula, gently press bread to cover with milk mixture. Cover, and let stand 30 minutes.

Bake, uncovered, until puffed and golden brown and a knife inserted near center comes out clean, approximately 55 minutes. Let stand 30 minutes.

FOR SAUCE: In a large saucepan, bring brown sugar, butter, bourbon, ⅓ cup water, and salt to a boil, stirring constantly. Reduce heat to low. Simmer 5 minutes, stirring constantly. Stir in pecans. Serve warm with bread pudding.

BUTTERSCOTCH TART

YIELD: 1 (10-INCH) TART

CRUST

1½	cups all-purpose flour
⅓	cup finely ground pecans
¼	cup confectioners' sugar
¼	teaspoon salt
½	cup unsalted butter, softened
1	tablespoon browned butter, softened (see note)
1	large egg yolk
1	tablespoon heavy whipping cream

SAUCE

¾	cup butterscotch morsels
¼	cup heavy whipping cream
1	tablespoon light corn syrup

FILLING

2	(3.4-ounce) boxes butterscotch-flavored instant pudding and pie filling
2¾	cups cold half-and-half
1	teaspoon vanilla extract

Garnish: chopped chocolate

FOR CRUST: In the work bowl of a food processor, combine flour, pecans, confectioners' sugar, and salt. Pulse until combined. Add butters, egg yolk, and cream, pulsing until a dough forms. Shape into a disk. Cover with plastic wrap, and refrigerate 2 hours.

Preheat oven to 350°.

On a lightly floured surface, roll dough into a 12-inch circle. Transfer to a 10-inch round removable-bottom tart pan. Press into bottom and up sides, trimming edges as needed. Prick bottom and sides with a fork 10 times. Top with a piece of parchment paper, letting ends extend over edges of pan. Add pie weights.

Bake until golden brown, approximately 30 minutes. Carefully remove paper and weights. Let cool 30 minutes.

FOR SAUCE: In a small saucepan, combine butterscotch morsels, cream, and syrup. Cook over medium-low heat, whisking constantly until smooth. Let cool 15 minutes. Spread approximately ½ cup sauce in bottom of prepared crust. Place in freezer while preparing filling. Set remaining sauce aside.

FOR FILLING: In a large bowl, combine pudding mix, half-and-half, and vanilla. Beat at medium-high speed with an electric mixer until set, approximately 2 minutes. Pour mixture into prepared crust, smoothing top with an offset spatula. Refrigerate until set, approximately 2 hours.

Carefully remove tart from pan. Drizzle with remaining sauce, and garnish with chopped chocolate, if desired. Cover, and refrigerate up to 3 days.

 Note: To make browned butter, melt ½ cup butter in a stainless steel skillet over medium heat. Cook, stirring constantly, until butter becomes honey colored and has a nutty aroma, 8 to 10 minutes. Remove from heat to avoid burning. Strain through a fine-mesh sieve. Refrigerate just until set. Let soften before using.

COCONUT-LEMON PIE

YIELD: 1 (9-INCH) PIE

CRUST

1⅓ cups all-purpose flour

1 tablespoon sugar

½ teaspoon salt

3 tablespoons cold unsalted butter, cut into pieces

3 tablespoons all-vegetable shortening

4 to 5 tablespoons ice water

FILLING

½ cup sugar

½ cup all-purpose flour

2¼ cups whole milk

4 large egg yolks

1 cup sweetened flaked coconut

3 tablespoons butter

2 teaspoons lemon zest

2 tablespoons fresh lemon juice

MERINGUE

1 cup sugar

4 large egg whites, at room temperature

Garnish: toasted sweetened flaked coconut

FOR CRUST: In a large bowl, stir together flour, sugar, and salt. Using a pastry blender, cut in butter and shortening until mixture resembles coarse crumbs. Gradually sprinkle 4 to 5 tablespoons ice water over flour mixture, stirring until moistened. Shape dough into a disk. Cover with plastic wrap, and refrigerate 1 hour.

Preheat oven to 400°. On a lightly floured surface, roll dough into a 12-inch circle. Transfer to a 9-inch pie plate, pressing into bottom and up sides. Fold edges under, and crimp as desired. Prick bottom and sides with a fork 10 times. Top with a piece of parchment paper, letting ends extend over edges of plate. Add pie weights. Bake until edges begin to brown, approximately 20 minutes. Reduce oven temperature to 375°. Carefully remove paper and weights. Bake until lightly browned, approximately 20 minutes more. Let cool completely on a wire rack.

FOR FILLING: In a large saucepan, combine sugar and flour. Whisk in milk. Cook over medium heat, stirring constantly, until thick and bubbly. Remove from heat. In a medium bowl, place egg yolks. Gradually add 1 cup hot milk mixture, whisking to combine. Add egg yolk mixture to remaining hot milk mixture in saucepan. Cook over medium heat, stirring constantly, until thick and bubbly. Remove from heat. Add coconut, butter, and lemon zest and juice. Stir until butter melts. Spoon mixture in prepared crust. Place plastic wrap directly on surface of filling. Refrigerate until chilled.

FOR MERINGUE: In the top half of a double boiler, whisk together sugar and egg whites. Place over simmering water, whisking constantly until sugar dissolves and egg whites are warm, 3 to 4 minutes. In the bowl of a stand mixer using the whisk attachment, beat egg white mixture at low speed 2 minutes. Increase speed to high, and beat until stiff peaks form and mixture cools, approximately 6 minutes. Remove plastic wrap from filling. Spoon egg white mixture onto center of pie, spreading to within 1 inch of crust. Using your fingers, pull meringue into tall peaks. Using a kitchen torch, lightly brown top of meringue. Garnish with coconut, if desired.

COOKIES, CANDIES, and BARS

PEANUT BUTTER COOKIES

YIELD: APPROXIMATELY 3 DOZEN COOKIES

¼ cup butter-flavored all-vegetable shortening

¾ cup sugar, divided

½ cup firmly packed light brown sugar

1 teaspoon vanilla extract

¾ cup creamy peanut butter

1 large egg

1½ cups all-purpose flour

1 teaspoon baking soda

½ teaspoon salt

2 tablespoons heavy whipping cream

1 tablespoon ground cinnamon

Preheat oven to 350°. Line rimmed baking sheets with parchment paper. Set aside.

In a large bowl, beat shortening, ½ cup sugar, brown sugar, and vanilla at medium-high speed with an electric mixer until fluffy, stopping occasionally to scrape sides of bowl. Add peanut butter, beating until smooth. Add egg, beating to combine.

In a medium bowl, whisk together flour, baking soda, and salt. Reduce mixer speed to low. Add flour mixture to shortening mixture in thirds, beating well after each addition. Add cream, beating to combine.

In a small bowl, stir together remaining ¼ cup sugar and cinnamon. Scoop dough by heaping tablespoonfuls. Using hands, roll into balls. Place balls in cinnamon sugar, tossing to coat. Place on prepared pans, spacing 2 inches apart. Using a fork, press each ball to approximately ½ inch thick, making a crosshatch design.

Bake until edges are just beginning to brown, 12 to 15 minutes. Let cool on pans 5 minutes. Remove from pans, and let cool completely on wire racks. Store in an airtight container up to 5 days.

HANDMADE
with love

PECAN-TOFFEE SHORTBREAD

YIELD: APPROXIMATELY 3 DOZEN COOKIES

1	cup butter, softened
2	cups all-purpose flour
½	cup confectioners' sugar
¼	cup cornstarch
2	tablespoons heavy whipping cream
1	teaspoon vanilla extract
1	cup finely chopped pecans
1½	cups semisweet chocolate morsels, melted
½	cup chocolate-covered toffee bits

In a large bowl, beat butter at medium speed with an electric mixer until creamy. In a medium bowl, combine flour, confectioners' sugar, and cornstarch. Add flour mixture, cream, vanilla, and pecans to butter, beating until well combined. Cover dough with plastic wrap, and refrigerate 2 hours.

Preheat oven to 350°. Line baking sheets with parchment paper. Set aside.

On a lightly floured surface, roll dough to ¼ inch thick. Using a 2-inch square cutter, cut out dough, rerolling scraps twice. Place on prepared pans, spacing 1 inch apart.

Bake until lightly browned, 12 to 14 minutes. Let cool on pans 5 minutes. Remove from pans, and let cool completely on wire racks. (Set pans aside, and let cool.) Dip half of each cookie in melted chocolate, and return to prepared pans.

Sprinkle with toffee bits. Let stand until chocolate is set, approximately 1 hour. Store in an airtight container up to 5 days.

CHOCOLATE CHUNK COOKIES

YIELD: APPROXIMATELY 2 DOZEN COOKIES

1¾ cups white whole-wheat flour

¾ teaspoon ground cinnamon

½ teaspoon ground ginger

½ teaspoon baking soda

¼ teaspoon ground allspice

⅛ teaspoon ground cloves

14 tablespoons unsalted butter, softened and divided

¾ cup firmly packed dark brown sugar

½ cup sugar

2 teaspoons vanilla extract

1 teaspoon kosher salt

1 large egg

1 large egg yolk

1 cup semisweet chocolate chunks

½ cup toasted pecans, finely chopped

Preheat oven to 375°. Line 2 baking sheets with parchment paper. Set aside.

In a medium bowl, whisk together flour, cinnamon, ginger, baking soda, allspice, and cloves.

In a small skillet, melt 10 tablespoons butter over medium-high heat. Cook until butter is golden brown, 3 to 4 minutes. Transfer to a large bowl. Add remaining 4 tablespoons butter, stirring until melted.

Add sugars, vanilla, and salt, stirring to combine. Add egg and egg yolk, whisking well until combined, 3 to 4 minutes. Add flour mixture to butter mixture, stirring until combined. Add chocolate and pecans, stirring just until combined.

Scoop dough by heaping tablespoonfuls. Using hands, roll into balls. Place on prepared pans, spacing 2 inches apart.

Bake until edges are golden brown, 8 to 14 minutes. Let cool on pans 5 minutes. Remove from pans, and let cool completely on wire racks.

BUTTERSCOTCH-WALNUT BLONDIES

YIELD: APPROXIMATELY 9 BARS

1   **cup unsalted butter, melted and cooled slightly**
1½ **cups firmly packed light brown sugar**
2   **large eggs**
2   **teaspoons vanilla extract**
2   **cups all-purpose flour**
1   **teaspoon baking powder**
1   **teaspoon kosher salt**
¾   **cup butterscotch morsels**
¾   **cup chopped walnuts**

Preheat oven to 350°. Spray an 8x8-inch baking pan with nonstick baking spray with flour. Set aside.

In a medium bowl, whisk together melted butter and brown sugar until smooth. Whisk in eggs and vanilla.

In another medium bowl, whisk together flour, baking powder, and salt. Gradually add egg mixture to flour mixture, stirring to combine. Gently stir in butterscotch and walnuts. Spread batter in prepared pan, smoothing top with an offset spatula.

Bake until golden brown and a wooden pick inserted in center comes out clean, approximately 20 minutes.

Let cool completely on a wire rack. Cut into bars.

HOT CHOCOLATE COOKIES

YIELD: APPROXIMATELY 2 DOZEN COOKIES

½   cup unsalted butter, softened
1   cup sugar, divided
1   large egg
1¼   cups all-purpose flour
½   cup powdered milk
¼   cup natural unsweetened cocoa
     powder
1   teaspoon baking soda
½   teaspoon kosher salt
1   teaspoon vanilla extract
1   teaspoon ground cinnamon
12   large marshmallows, cut in half

Preheat oven to 350°. Line 2 baking sheets with parchment paper. Set aside.

In a large bowl, beat butter and ⅔ cup sugar at medium speed with an electric mixer until fluffy, stopping occasionally to scrape sides of bowl. Add egg, beating until combined.

In a medium bowl, whisk together flour, powdered milk, cocoa, baking soda, and salt. Gradually add flour mixture to butter mixture, beating until well combined. Beat in vanilla.

In a small bowl, stir together remaining ⅓ cup sugar and cinnamon. Scoop dough by heaping tablespoonfuls. Using hands, roll into balls. Roll balls in sugar mixture. Place on prepared pans, spacing 2 inches apart.

Bake until set, approximately 8 minutes. Working quickly, press 1 marshmallow half, cut side down, in center of each cookie.

Set oven to broil. Watching carefully, broil 5 inches from heat until marshmallows are lightly toasted, approximately 3 minutes. Let cool on pans 5 minutes. Remove from pans, and let cool completely on wire racks. Store in an airtight container up to 5 days.

TURTLE FUDGE

$2^{3}/_{4}$ cups sugar

$^{3}/_{4}$ cup whole milk

$^{3}/_{4}$ cup butter-flavored all-vegetable shortening

8 (1-ounce) squares semisweet baking chocolate, chopped

4 (1-ounce) squares unsweetened baking chocolate, chopped

1 (7-ounce) jar marshmallow crème, such as Marshmallow Fluff

2 teaspoons vanilla extract

1 teaspoon sea salt, divided

28 chocolate-covered caramel candies, cut in half, such as Rolos

1 cup toasted pecans, chopped

Line a 9x9-inch baking pan with aluminum foil, letting ends of foil extend over edges of pan approximately 2 inches. Set aside.

In a large saucepan, combine sugar, milk, and shortening. Cook over high heat, stirring constantly, until a candy thermometer reads 234°, approximately 4 minutes. Remove from heat. Add chocolates, marshmallow crème, vanilla, and $^{3}/_{4}$ teaspoon salt, stirring until smooth. Fold in candies. Spread in prepared pan, smoothing top with an offset spatula. Top with pecans and remaining $^{1}/_{4}$ teaspoon salt. Let cool completely.

Lift edges of foil to remove from pan. Cut into small squares. Store in an airtight container up to 5 days.

CLASSIC DIVINITY

YIELD: APPROXIMATELY 2 DOZEN PIECES

2   large egg whites, at room
     temperature
2½   cups sugar
½   cup water
½   cup light corn syrup
½   teaspoon kosher salt
24   pecan halves

Line 2 baking sheets with parchment paper. Set aside.

In a large bowl, beat egg whites at high speed with an electric mixer until stiff peaks form. Set aside.

In a medium saucepan, combine sugar, ½ cup water, syrup, and salt. Cook over medium-high heat, stirring occasionally, until a candy thermometer reads 248°.

With mixer on low speed, gradually add half of sugar mixture to egg white mixture. Increase speed to high; beat approximately 5 minutes.

Meanwhile, cook remaining sugar mixture over medium-high heat until a candy thermometer reads 272°. With mixer on high speed, gradually add sugar mixture to egg whites. Beat until mixture begins to lose its gloss and starts to thicken, 4 to 5 minutes.

Working very quickly, drop mixture by heaping tablespoonfuls onto prepared pans. Immediately top with pecan halves. Let cool until set. Store in an airtight container up to 1 week.

RED VELVET PEPPERMINT COOKIES

YIELD: APPROXIMATELY 28 COOKIES

¾ cup butter, softened and divided

1 cup sugar

1 large egg

1½ cups self-rising flour

3½ tablespoons natural unsweetened cocoa powder

2 teaspoons red food coloring

1 teaspoon distilled white vinegar

1 teaspoon vanilla extract

¾ teaspoon peppermint extract

4 ounces cream cheese, softened

2 cups confectioners' sugar

½ cup crushed soft peppermints

Preheat oven to 375°. Line baking sheets with parchment paper. Set aside.

In a large bowl, beat ½ cup butter and sugar at medium speed with an electric mixer until fluffy, stopping occasionally to scrape sides of bowl. Add egg, beating until combined.

In a medium bowl, whisk together flour and cocoa. Add flour mixture to butter mixture, beating until combined. Add food coloring, vinegar, and extracts, beating until combined. Spoon dough by tablespoonfuls onto prepared pans, spacing 2 inches apart.

Bake until almost firm, approximately 10 minutes. Let cool on pans 5 minutes. Remove from pans, and let cool completely on wire racks.

In a large bowl, beat remaining ¼ cup butter and cream cheese at medium speed with an electric mixer until smooth. Gradually add confectioners' sugar, beating until combined. Spread cream cheese mixture over cookies; sprinkle with peppermint. Store unfrosted cookies in an airtight container up to 2 days.

FIG BARS

YIELD: APPROXIMATELY 16 BARS

3   cups chopped dried figs
1   cup water
½   cup dry red wine
¼   cup sugar
½   teaspoon orange zest
⅛   teaspoon kosher salt
¾   cup unsalted butter
1   cup firmly packed light brown
    sugar
1¾ cups all-purpose flour
1¼ teaspoons kosher salt
½   teaspoon baking soda
1   cup old-fashioned oats
½   cup finely chopped pecans

Preheat oven to 375°. Spray a 13x9-inch baking dish with nonstick cooking spray. Set aside.

In a medium saucepan, bring figs, 1 cup water, wine, sugar, zest, and salt to a boil over medium-high heat, stirring constantly. Reduce heat to medium-low, and cook, stirring occasionally, until mixture is thickened and reduced to 2½ cups, approximately 10 minutes. Let cool completely. Set aside.

In a large bowl, beat butter and brown sugar at medium speed with an electric mixer until fluffy, stopping occasionally to scrape sides of bowl. In another bowl, stir together flour, salt, and baking soda. With mixer on low speed, slowly add flour mixture to butter mixture, beating to combine. (Mixture will be crumbly.) Gradually add oats and pecans, beating just until combined.

Using the bottom of a measuring cup, press half of crust mixture into bottom of prepared pan. Gently spread fig mixture evenly over crust. Sprinkle with remaining crust mixture, pressing lightly.

Bake until golden brown, 25 to 30 minutes. Let cool slightly. Cut into bars.

PRALINES

YIELD: APPROXIMATELY 2 DOZEN PRALINES

1   cup sugar

1   cup firmly packed light brown sugar

½   cup heavy whipping cream

¼   teaspoon baking soda

2   tablespoons unsalted butter

1   teaspoon vanilla extract

2   cups pecan halves

Line a baking sheet with parchment paper. Set aside.

In a medium saucepan, bring sugars, cream, and baking soda to a boil. Cook, stirring occasionally, until a candy thermometer reads 240°. Remove from heat; stir in butter and vanilla. Quickly add pecans, stirring vigorously until mixture thickens and loses some of its shine, 1 to 2 minutes.

Working quickly, drop mixture by heaping tablespoonfuls onto prepared pan. (If mixture hardens, add 1 tablespoon hot water at a time to return to a spoonable consistency.)

Let cool until hardened, approximately 10 minutes. Store in an airtight container up to 1 week.

CHERRY-APRICOT CRUMBLE BARS

YIELD: APPROXIMATELY 1 DOZEN BARS

3   cups quick-cooking oats (not instant)
1   cup all-purpose flour
1   cup sugar
½   teaspoon baking soda
¼   teaspoon salt
⅛   teaspoon ground nutmeg
¾   cup butter, melted
1   (21-ounce) can cherry pie filling
⅔   cup chopped dried apricots

Preheat oven to 350°. Line a 13x9-inch baking pan with aluminum foil, letting ends of foil extend over edges of pan approximately 2 inches.

In a large bowl, combine oats, flour, sugar, baking soda, salt, and nutmeg. Add melted butter, stirring to combine. Reserve 1 cup crumble mixture. Using the bottom of a measuring cup, press remaining mixture into bottom of prepared pan.

Bake until set, 12 to 14 minutes.

In a small bowl, combine pie filling and apricots. Gently spread mixture evenly over prepared crust. Sprinkle with reserved 1 cup crumble mixture.

Bake until lightly browned and bubbly, 30 to 35 minutes. Let cool completely on a wire rack. Lift edges of foil to remove from pan. Cut into bars.

MISSISSIPPI MUD BARS

YIELD: 10 TO 12 SERVINGS

BARS

1 cup butter, melted

2 cups sugar

⅓ cup natural unsweetened cocoa powder

3 large eggs

1 teaspoon vanilla extract

¼ teaspoon salt

2 cups all-purpose flour

2 cups toasted pecans, chopped and divided

1 (10.5-ounce) bag miniature marshmallows

GLAZE

½ cup butter

½ cup heavy whipping cream

1 cup semisweet chocolate morsels

Preheat oven to 350°. Spray a 13x9-inch baking pan with nonstick baking spray with flour. Set aside.

FOR BARS: In a large bowl, combine melted butter, sugar, cocoa, eggs, vanilla, and salt. Beat at medium speed with an electric mixer until combined. Gradually add flour, beating to combine. Stir in 1 cup pecans. Spread batter evenly in prepared pan.

Bake until a wooden pick inserted in center comes out clean, 20 to 30 minutes. Top with marshmallows. Return to oven, and bake until marshmallows are lightly browned, 5 to 7 minutes. Let cool 5 minutes.

FOR GLAZE: In a medium saucepan, cook butter and cream over medium heat, stirring until butter melts. Add chocolate, stirring until melted and smooth.

Sprinkle remaining 1 cup pecans over marshmallows; drizzle with glaze. Let cool completely, and cut into bars.

BACON-PECAN SANDIES

YIELD: APPROXIMATELY 3 DOZEN COOKIES

5   slices bacon

1   cup pecan pieces

¾   cup unsalted butter, softened

½   cup sugar

1¾   cups all-purpose flour

⅛   teaspoon salt

½   teaspoon baking powder

1   teaspoon vanilla extract

20   (1-ounce) squares semisweet
      chocolate, chopped

In a large skillet, cook bacon over medium heat until crisp. Remove bacon using a slotted spoon. Let cool; crumble. Reserve 1 tablespoon rendered bacon fat; transfer to a small bowl. Cover, and refrigerate until firm.

In the work bowl of a food processor, combine half of crumbled bacon and pecans; pulse until finely ground, 6 or 7 times.

In a large bowl, beat chilled bacon fat, butter, and sugar at medium speed with an electric mixer until creamy. Add flour, salt, and baking powder; beat on low speed until combined, stopping occasionally to scrape sides of bowl. Add pecan mixture and vanilla; beat until combined.

Divide dough in half. Using floured hands, roll each half into an 8½-inch log. Wrap each log tightly in wax paper. Refrigerate until firm, approximately 1 hour.

Preheat oven to 350°. Line baking sheets with parchment paper.

Unwrap 1 portion of dough. Using a sharp knife, trim ¼ inch from each end of log, and discard. Cut dough into approximately ⅜-inch-thick slices. Place slices 1 inch apart on prepared pans.

Bake until lightly browned around edges, approximately 12 minutes. Let cool on pans 5 minutes. Remove from pans, and let cool completely on wire racks. Repeat procedure with remaining dough.

Melt chocolate according to package directions; let cool slightly. Line 2 baking sheets with wax paper. Spoon 1 tablespoon melted chocolate onto prepared pan. Top with 1 cookie; lightly press until chocolate extends approximately ¼ inch around edge of cookie. Spoon approximately ¼ teaspoon melted chocolate on top of cookie. Place 2 bacon crumbles in center of chocolate. Repeat procedure with remaining cookies, melted chocolate, and bacon. Set aside in a cool place until chocolate is thoroughly set and cookies can be easily removed from wax paper, 3 to 4 hours.

WHITE CHOCOLATE-CRANBERRY TOFFEE

YIELD: APPROXIMATELY 4½ DOZEN PIECES

54	saltine crackers
1	cup butter
1	cup firmly packed light brown sugar
1	(14-ounce) can sweetened condensed milk
6	(1-ounce) squares white chocolate, finely chopped
1	cup chopped pecans
½	cup chopped sweetened dried cranberries

Preheat oven to 425°. Line a 15x10-inch jelly-roll pan with heavy-duty aluminum foil. Spray foil with nonstick cooking spray.

Arrange crackers in a single layer on prepared pan.

In a medium saucepan, bring butter and brown sugar to a boil over medium-high heat. Cook 2 minutes. Remove from heat, and stir in condensed milk. Pour mixture over crackers.

Bake 10 minutes. Sprinkle with chopped white chocolate. Let stand 1 to 2 minutes to soften. Using a small offset spatula, spread softened chocolate in an even layer. Sprinkle with pecans and cranberries. Let cool completely.

Break into pieces. Store in an airtight container up to 5 days.

ICEBOX DESSERTS

TIRAMISÙ ICEBOX CAKE

YIELD: APPROXIMATELY 10 SERVINGS

1   (15.25-ounce) box white cake mix,
    such as Pillsbury
1   (3.4-ounce) box vanilla-flavored
    instant pudding and pie filling
4   teaspoons natural unsweetened
    cocoa powder, divided
4   teaspoons instant espresso
    powder, divided
1½ cups heavy whipping cream
½   cup confectioners' sugar
½   cup sour cream

Preheat oven to 350°. Spray bottom only of a 13x9-inch baking dish with nonstick baking spray with flour. Set aside.

Prepare cake mix according to package directions for whole-egg recipe. Pour batter into prepared dish. Bake according to package directions. Let cool 15 minutes.

Prepare pudding according to package directions. Using the handle of a wooden spoon, poke holes in warm cake, making sure handle does not touch bottom of pan. Spread pudding over cake. Sprinkle with 2 teaspoons cocoa and 2 teaspoons espresso.

In a large bowl, beat cream, confectioners' sugar, and sour cream at high speed with an electric mixer until stiff peaks form. Spread over cake. Sprinkle with remaining 2 teaspoons cocoa and 2 teaspoons espresso. Cover, and refrigerate at least 2 hours or up to 2 days.

SWEET TEA ICE CREAM

YIELD: APPROXIMATELY 2 QUARTS

4 cups half-and-half

1 cup firmly packed light brown sugar

¼ cup fresh lemon juice

2 family-size tea bags

½ vanilla bean, split lengthwise and seeds scraped and reserved

2 teaspoons vanilla extract

12 large egg yolks

Garnish: fresh blackberries, fresh mint, fresh lavender

In a medium saucepan, combine half-and-half, brown sugar, lemon juice, tea bags, reserved vanilla bean seeds, and extract. Heat over medium-high heat until mixture just begins to boil. Remove from heat.

In a medium bowl, whisk egg yolks until smooth. Gradually add 1 cup half-and-half mixture to egg yolks, whisking constantly. Add another 1 cup half-and-half mixture, whisking to combine. Transfer mixture to saucepan.

Cook over medium-high heat, stirring constantly, until mixture thickens and coats the back of a wooden spoon or a candy thermometer reads 170°. Pour mixture through a fine-mesh sieve into a stainless-steel bowl set over a bowl of ice water. Let cool completely, stirring often. Cover, and refrigerate until completely cold.

Freeze mixture in an ice cream maker according to manufacturer's instructions. If a firmer texture is desired, transfer to an airtight container, and freeze until firm, approximately 2 hours or up to 3 weeks. Garnish with blackberries, mint, and lavender, if desired.

COCONUT CAKE CHEESECAKE

YIELD: 8 TO 10 SERVINGS

CRUST

2	cups graham cracker crumbs
1	cup sweetened flaked coconut
½	cup butter, melted

FILLING

2	(8-ounce) packages cream cheese, softened
1	cup sugar
3	large eggs
2	cups sour cream
1	teaspoon fresh lime juice
1	teaspoon vanilla extract

TOPPING

½	cup sweetened condensed milk
¼	cup coconut milk
1¼	cups sweetened flaked coconut
½	teaspoon vanilla extract

Preheat oven to 325°.

FOR CRUST: In a medium bowl, stir together graham cracker crumbs, coconut, and melted butter. Using the bottom of a measuring cup, press evenly into bottom and up sides of an 8-inch springform pan. Refrigerate 10 minutes.

FOR FILLING: In a large bowl, beat cream cheese and sugar at medium speed with an electric mixer until fluffy. Add eggs, one at a time, beating just until combined after each addition. Add sour cream, lime juice, and vanilla, beating until well combined. Pour into prepared crust.

Wrap aluminum foil tightly around bottom of springform pan. Place wrapped pan in a large roasting pan. Add boiling water to roasting pan until water reaches halfway up sides of wrapped pan.

Bake until center of cheesecake is set but jiggles slightly in the middle, approximately 1 hour and 15 minutes. Carefully remove cheesecake from roasting pan, and let cool completely in pan on a wire rack. Refrigerate overnight.

FOR TOPPING: In a small bowl, stir together condensed milk, coconut milk, coconut, and vanilla. Pour over cheesecake. Serve immediately.

COOKIES AND CREAM SHEET CAKE

YIELD: 10 TO 12 SERVINGS

3½ cups finely crushed chocolate sandwich cookies, such as Oreos (about 36 cookies)

6 tablespoons unsalted butter, melted

½ gallon cookies and cream ice cream, softened

1½ cups broken chocolate sandwich cookies (about 14 cookies)

3 cups heavy whipping cream

½ cup sugar

Garnish: broken chocolate sandwich cookies

Preheat oven to 350°. Line a 13x9-inch baking dish with parchment paper, letting ends extend over edges of dish.

In a medium bowl, stir together crushed cookies and melted butter until combined. Using the bottom of a measuring cup, press mixture into bottom of prepared dish.

Bake until set, approximately 12 minutes. Let cool completely on a wire rack.

In a large bowl, stir together ice cream and broken cookies until combined. Spread mixture into cooled crust, smoothing top with an offset spatula. Freeze until solid, at least 4 hours.

In a large bowl, beat cream and sugar at high speed with an electric mixer until stiff peaks form. Top cake with whipped cream, and garnish with cookies, if desired.

ICEBOX ITALIAN CREAM CAKE

YIELD: APPROXIMATELY 12 SERVINGS

2 (3.4-ounce) boxes vanilla-flavored instant pudding and pie filling
1 (8-ounce) package cream cheese, softened
½ cup butter, softened
2 cups heavy whipping cream
1⅓ cups confectioners' sugar
1 teaspoon vanilla extract
3 (3-ounce) packages soft ladyfingers, torn into pieces
½ cup sweetened flaked coconut
½ cup toasted pecans, chopped

Prepare pudding according to package directions. Set aside.

In a large bowl, beat cream cheese and butter at medium speed with an electric mixer until smooth. Add cream and confectioners' sugar. Beat until mixture begins to thicken. Increase speed to high; beat until stiff peaks form. Beat in vanilla.

In a 13x9-inch dish, layer half of ladyfingers. Spread half of pudding over ladyfingers. Repeat procedure once. Gently spread cream cheese mixture over pudding. Sprinkle with coconut and pecans. Cover, and refrigerate at least 1 hour or up to 3 hours.

STRAWBERRY-BUTTERMILK ICE CREAM SUNDAES

YIELD: APPROXIMATELY 6 SERVINGS

ICE CREAM

3   large egg yolks, lightly beaten
½   cup sugar
⅛   teaspoon salt
2   cups heavy whipping cream
1   cup whole buttermilk
1   teaspoon vanilla extract
1½   cups halved fresh strawberries
⅓   cup strawberry preserves

SUNDAES

1½   cups strawberry syrup,
     such as Smucker's
Ice cream
1   cup quartered fresh strawberries
½   cup chopped pecans, toasted
1½   cups sweetened whipped cream

FOR ICE CREAM: In a large bowl, whisk together egg yolks, sugar, and salt. Set aside.

In a medium saucepan, combine cream, buttermilk, and vanilla. Bring to a simmer over medium heat, stirring occasionally. Gradually add hot cream mixture to egg yolk mixture, whisking to combine. Return mixture to saucepan. Cook over medium heat, stirring constantly, until mixture thickens and coats the back of a wooden spoon. Pour mixture through a fine-mesh sieve into a stainless-steel bowl set over a bowl of ice water. Let cool completely, stirring often. Cover, and refrigerate until completely cold.

Freeze mixture in an ice cream maker according to manufacturer's instructions. Spoon into an airtight container.

In the container of a blender, combine strawberries and preserves; pulse until strawberries are coarsely chopped, approximately 4 times. Fold into ice cream mixture. Cover, and freeze until firm, approximately 2 hours or up to 3 weeks.

FOR SUNDAES: In 6 dessert glasses or dishes, layer syrup, ice cream, strawberries, pecans, and whipped cream as desired.

BANANA PUDDING BARS

YIELD: APPROXIMATELY 1½ DOZEN BARS

CRUST

2	cups graham cracker crumbs
1½	cups gingersnap cookie crumbs
½	cup butter, melted

FILLING

3	cups whole milk, divided
1½	cups fresh banana purée (2 to 3 medium bananas)
1	cup sugar, divided
2	teaspoons vanilla extract
3	teaspoons unflavored gelatin
8	large egg yolks
½	cup all-purpose flour

TOPPING

1½	cups heavy whipping cream
¼	cup confectioners' sugar

Garnish: mini vanilla wafers

Preheat oven to 350°. Line a 13x9-inch baking pan with parchment paper, letting ends extend over edges of pan.

FOR CRUST: In a medium bowl, stir together graham cracker crumbs, gingersnap crumbs, and melted butter. Using the bottom of a measuring cup, press into bottom of prepared pan.

Bake until set, approximately 10 minutes. Remove from oven, and let cool on a wire rack.

FOR FILLING: In a medium saucepan, combine 2¾ cups milk, banana purée, ¾ cup sugar, and vanilla. Cook over medium heat, whisking frequently, until mixture boils. Remove from heat.

In a small bowl, combine remaining ¼ cup milk and gelatin. Let stand 5 minutes. Meanwhile, in a medium bowl, whisk together egg yolks, remaining ¼ cup sugar, and flour until smooth. Set aside.

Add gelatin mixture to milk mixture, whisking to combine.

Gradually add 1 cup hot milk mixture to yolk mixture, whisking constantly. Add egg mixture to milk mixture, whisking to combine. Cook, stirring constantly, over medium-high heat, until mixture begins to thicken. Gently boil 2 minutes. Remove from heat, and strain through a fine-mesh sieve into prepared crust. Smooth top with an offset spatula. Let cool to room temperature. Cover, and refrigerate at least 6 hours.

FOR TOPPING: In a medium bowl, combine cream and confectioners' sugar. Beat at medium-high speed with an electric mixer until medium peaks form. Spread over filling. Cut into bars. Garnish each bar with a mini wafer, if desired. Cover, and refrigerate up to 5 days.

CHEERWINE ICE CREAM

YIELD: APPROXIMATELY 6 SERVINGS

2   cups heavy whipping cream
1   (12-ounce) bottle Cheerwine
½   cup sugar, divided
5   large egg yolks
⅛   teaspoon salt

In a large saucepan, bring cream, Cheerwine, and ¼ cup sugar just to a simmer over medium heat. (Do not let mixture boil.)

In a medium bowl, whisk together remaining ¼ cup sugar and egg yolks. Gradually add warm cream mixture to egg mixture, whisking constantly. Transfer mixture to saucepan.

Cook, stirring constantly, over medium heat, until mixture thickens and coats the back of a wooden spoon or a candy thermometer reads 170°, approximately 6 minutes. Stir in salt. Pour mixture through a fine-mesh sieve into a stainless-steel bowl set over a bowl of ice water. Let cool completely, stirring often. Cover, and refrigerate until completely cold.

Freeze mixture in an ice cream maker according to manufacturer's instructions. If a firmer texture is desired, transfer to an airtight container, and freeze until firm, approximately 2 hours or up to 3 weeks.

BROWNIE AND PISTACHIO ICE CREAM CAKE

YIELD: 6 TO 8 SERVINGS

1   (10-ounce) package bittersweet chocolate morsels
1   cup unsalted butter
1   cup sugar
1   cup firmly packed light brown sugar
2   teaspoons vanilla extract
4   large eggs, lightly beaten
2   cups all-purpose flour
1   teaspoon kosher salt
½   teaspoon baking powder
1   cup semisweet chocolate morsels
2   pints pistachio ice cream, softened
1   cup heavy whipping cream
⅓   cup finely chopped pistachios

Preheat oven to 350°. Line an 18x13-inch rimmed baking sheet with parchment paper. Spray with nonstick cooking spray. Set aside.

In the top half of a double boiler, melt bittersweet chocolate and butter. Remove from heat. Stir in sugars, vanilla, and eggs.

In a medium bowl, stir together flour, salt, and baking powder. Gradually add flour mixture to chocolate mixture, stirring just until combined. Fold in semisweet chocolate. Spread batter evenly in prepared pan.

Bake until a wooden pick inserted in center comes out clean, 15 to 20 minutes. Let cool completely on a wire rack.

Line an 8½x4½-inch loaf pan with parchment paper, letting ends extend over edges of pan.

Using bottom of pan as a guide, cut 3 rectangles from brownies. (You will have leftover brownies.) Place 1 brownie rectangle in bottom of prepared pan; spread with 1 pint softened ice cream, smoothing top with an offset spatula. Repeat procedure once; top with remaining brownie rectangle, pressing firmly. Cover loaf tightly with plastic wrap, and freeze overnight.

In a medium bowl, beat cream at high speed with an electric mixer until soft peaks form. Run a knife around edges of pan to release cake. Using paper as handles, remove cake from pan. Top with whipped cream, and sprinkle with pistachios.

Note: We used natural-colored Häagen-Dazs Pistachio Ice Cream.

PUMPKIN ICE CREAM

YIELD: APPROXIMATELY 4 SERVINGS

1½ cups whole milk

1 cup heavy whipping cream

⅔ cup sugar

¼ cup firmly packed light brown sugar

⅛ teaspoon salt

5 large egg yolks

1 (15-ounce) can pumpkin purée

2 teaspoons pumpkin pie spice

1 teaspoon vanilla extract

Garnish: purchased pecan brittle

In a medium saucepan, bring milk, cream, sugars, and salt to a simmer over medium heat, stirring occasionally.

In a medium bowl, place egg yolks. Gradually add half of hot milk mixture, whisking constantly. Transfer egg mixture to remaining milk mixture in saucepan, whisking to combine. Cook over medium heat, stirring constantly, until mixture thickens and coats the back of a wooden spoon or a candy thermometer reads 170°. Remove from heat; stir in pumpkin. Pour mixture through a fine-mesh sieve into a stainless-steel bowl set over a bowl of ice water. Stir in pumpkin pie spice and vanilla. Let cool completely, stirring often. Cover, and refrigerate until completely cold.

Freeze mixture in an ice cream maker according to manufacturer's instructions. If a firmer texture is desired, transfer to an airtight container, and freeze until firm, approximately 2 hours or up to 3 weeks. Serve with pecan brittle, if desired.

FROZEN STRAWBERRY YOGURT PIE

YIELD: 1 (10-INCH) PIE

CRUST

1	cup graham cracker crumbs
1	cup ground pretzels
1	cup sugar
½	cup butter, melted

FILLING

2½	cups chopped fresh strawberries
1	cup sugar
1	tablespoon finely chopped fresh thyme leaves
1	(8-ounce) package cream cheese, softened
1	(16-ounce) container vanilla yogurt
½	cup confectioners' sugar
1	(8-ounce) container frozen nondairy whipped topping, thawed

Garnish: fresh strawberries, fresh thyme

Spray a 10-inch springform pan with nonstick baking spray with flour. Line bottom with parchment paper, and spray with nonstick baking spray with flour. Set aside.

FOR CRUST: In a large bowl, combine graham cracker crumbs, pretzels, and sugar. Add melted butter, stirring to combine. Using the bottom of a measuring cup, press mixture into bottom of prepared pan. Place pan in freezer while preparing filling.

FOR FILLING: In the work bowl of a food processor, combine strawberries, sugar, and thyme. Pulse until smooth.

In another large bowl, beat cream cheese at high speed with an electric mixer until creamy, approximately 3 minutes. Add yogurt and confectioners' sugar, beating until smooth. Add strawberry mixture to yogurt mixture, beating to combine. Add whipped topping, beating until smooth.

Spoon mixture into prepared crust. Freeze 4 hours. Remove bottom and sides of pan. Garnish with strawberries and thyme, if desired. Cover, and freeze up to 1 week.

SALTED PEANUT BRITTLE MILKSHAKES

YIELD: APPROXIMATELY 4 SERVINGS

2 cups roasted salted peanuts

¾ cup sugar

¼ cup water

1 teaspoon fleur de sel or other flaked salt

4 cups vanilla ice cream

1 cup whole milk

½ cup creamy peanut butter

¼ cup malted milk powder

Sweetened whipped cream

Line a baking pan with parchment paper. Spread peanuts in an even layer. Set aside.

In a small saucepan, bring sugar and ¼ cup water to a simmer over medium-high heat, stirring just until sugar dissolves. Continue cooking, without stirring, until mixture is brown, approximately 7 minutes. Carefully pour mixture evenly over peanuts; sprinkle with salt. Let cool completely. Break into small pieces.

In the container of a blender, combine ice cream, milk, peanut butter, and malted milk powder. Blend until smooth.

Pour into glasses; top with whipped cream and peanut brittle pieces. Store leftover brittle in an airtight container up to 1 week.

INDEX